DEAR AUSTEN

DEAR AUSTEN

NINA BAWDEN

ISIS
LARGE PRINT
Oxford

First published in Great Britain 2005
by
Virago Press

Published in Large Print 2005 by ISIS Publishing Ltd.,
7 Centremead, Osney Mead, Oxford OX2 0ES
by arrangement with
Time Warner Book Group UK

British Library Cataloguing in Publication Data
Bawden, Nina, 1925–
    Dear Austen. – Large print ed.
    1. Bawden, Nina, 1925–
    2. Railroad accidents – England – Potter's Bar
    3. Railroad accidents – Investigation – England
    4. Large type books
    I. Title
    823.9'14

ISBN 0–7531–9338–8 (hb)
ISBN 0–7531–9339–6 (pb)

Printed and bound in Great Britain by
T. J. International Ltd., Padstow, Cornwall

To the memory of the seven people
who were killed at Potters Bar
and to the families and friends
they left behind them

Acknowledgements

George Huxley, whose railway expertise has been invaluable; Louise Christian, who fought so valiantly on behalf of the injured of Potters Bar; Stephen Wakelam and Lennie Goodings for their steadfast encouragement as I set about writing this book and the Squadron Leader who kept me alive to be able to write it; to David Hare, author of *The Permanent Way* and to Kika Markham, who impersonated me in the excellent polemical play. And of course, above all, to my family and my friends for their unfailing love and support.

Danielle Hope has had three collections of poetry, *Fairground of Madness*, *City Fox* and *The Stone Ship*, published by Rockingham Press. She was born in Lancashire and now lives near King's Cross railway station. The poem "Potters Bar" represents the poet's view.

POTTERS BAR (after Auden)

I

This is the accountant doubting the order
totting the costs of repairing disorder

faxing his boss for a second contractor
who passed it on to Bloggs of Little Senshester.

Meanwhile the link wore thin and malign
the deal discussed over turbot and wine

and no one saw the instructions in bold
the message said urgent, but no one was told.

Blogg's bolts will fix rotted joints
to let the train pass over the points.

II

King's Cross. Luggage wheels
squeal along platform ten. Passengers
bustle bags into carriages. Bicker over
who faces front or back. Unwrap newspapers
and chocolate muffins. A woman rustles
in Cellophane for three green apples.

Then a jolt and the journey begins.
Coffee spills on a smart tie
and announcements advertise
arrival times, breakfasts, and first class service.

III

Under the canal, above city routes
past crowded stations and late commuters
town gardens and dogs barking at home
then cattle lazing after milking's done.
Headlines digested, tired passengers doze
those still awake half watch the quickening scene
or make their calls, or type at computers,
the mobiles start ringing, work has begun.

And no one expected the connection to fail
no one expected the train could crash
with passengers spilled across the rails
and families clutching ripped cases.
The line silent with terror and death.

IV

How do we commemorate those who died?
The anniversary bell rings, incense in our eyes.
Politicians don sombre pressed faces.

No one knows who is to blame,
no one is eager to answer the whys.
No one expected so many could perish

because of no mend in a rickety place
because of a deal passed on over lunch
because of the fourth contractor's bad hunch?

Danielle Hope

ONE

They told me you were dead.

You know the rest of the poem. We were reared on the same literary fodder, you and I. As was my brother Robin who chose to read this poem at your funeral — that is, the family one, not the later and grander memorial that the BBC organised at St Martin's in Trafalgar Square.

> *They told me, Heraclitus, they told me you were dead . . .*

Naturally, I didn't believe it. That is, natural to begin with, when I was barely conscious in hospital, blurred and fuddled by morphia, and someone spoke to me from a great distance, the far end of a dark, hollow tunnel. *You have been in a train crash. Austen is dead.* It was a bad dream. I thought, *Wake up, you fool, that'll stop it.*

But there are times even now, more than a year later, when I still expect to hear your key in the door, hear your voice when the telephone rings. Above all, in

Greece this spring, after I had paid the tax on the apartment and was sitting in the main square of Nauplion to recover, I realised that I was not only expecting but positively and calmly *waiting* for you to come and join me for a drink and to hear about my comic adventures with the tax office. *Why you pay all? Better little now, little next year, and then, who knows? Government may change, no tax at all . . .*

You will know the tone in which this was said — the amazement of the Greek speaker, the disbelief; how foolishly perverse to attempt to pay a tax in full and on time! But it was even more foolish of me to sit in the town square afterwards, drinking an ouzo and waiting for you to turn up so that I could tell you about it: there would have been no tax to pay if you had not already been dead, leaving your half of our apartment to our daughter as our Athenian lawyer had advised when we bought it, explaining that in Greek inheritance law it is cheaper to leave property to one of your children, certainly much cheaper than leaving a house to a wife who can never be a true member of your blood family, perhaps even cheaper than leaving it to the Church, though I am not certain of that and do not intend to waste my time finding out. Research has never been much in my line, as you know, either out of laziness or — as I prefer to think — because of a dedicated commitment to a novelist's freedom. So this is to be a personal letter about the events as I see them, telling you what has happened since that bloody accident on 10 May 2002 to all those who loved you and to some of the other stupidly trusting passengers whose lives were ended or destroyed. A year after they killed you, the contractor who was supposed to maintain that stretch of railway track declared a profit of sixty-seven million pounds.

It was that announcement in the business pages that finally decided me to think about writing to you. It clinched an impulse that had seized me a few weeks earlier when our daughter found a bunch of fragile and yellowing letters that you had hidden away at the back of that inaccessible (that is, inaccessible to a person of my height) top shelf of the cupboard in our bathroom; letters we had written to each other half a century ago when we were still married to other people, letters I thought we had agreed to destroy when you retired from the BBC and we were tidying our affairs before setting off on our travels, not wishing to leave anything behind that might present the children from both our marriages with difficulties or distress. Re-reading them was a curious consolation, an affectionate recognition of our silly young selves and the occasional unexpected reminder. I had forgotten, for example, among a good many other things, the extraordinary behaviour of your father, warning you when you went to boarding-school not to tell anyone that you were a Jew, and then, when he removed you for a couple of days to celebrate your bar mitzvah, advising you to pretend it was an Anglican confirmation. Mind you, knowing your father as I was to do until he died at the age of a hundred and two, a strong, gallant old man, still struggling to walk on his crutches in spite of his paralysed leg, I understand his behaviour — and him — much better now.

When he gave you that morally dubious advice he was drawing on his own experience of needing to "fit in". His parents had escaped from Russia in one of the pogroms at the end of the nineteenth century and gone to South Africa. In his twenties, just married to your mother who came from a rich family, he set off for London to make his own fortune. South Africa was too small, he told me once, he didn't want to be a big fish in a small pond; he wanted to be a mainstream journalist, a publisher, in one of the great cities of the world.

He was ambitious. He revered success as well as courting it — and not only monetary success. Of one of his younger brothers who died in his nineties, he said, "He never did have any stamina." And once, when I was dining alone with him at his club because you had a cold and didn't want to infect him, he said, of you, "Won't make old bones, that boy, will he?"

Do I half expect you to read this letter? I have never believed in Life After Death. I can see why it appeals — indeed, it appeals to me: the boat across the Styx, the reception committee on the far bank, the dear friends, the lost family, the tearful greetings, the laughter. But you are an atheist — struggling atheist would be more exact, perhaps — and I am what Archbishop Fisher once called, in an Easter service in Canterbury Cathedral, a sentimental Christian, the sort of person who thinks the Jesus story would be nice if it were true, and cheerfully conflates it with Greek myths. Before the coffin lid was closed and your broken body shuffled to the flames, your superstitious family, typically hedging their bets, put pennies for the ferryman into your jacket pocket.

I don't know. All I can be sure of is that some people, now several years dead, walk in and out of my mind, talking, arguing, smiling, exactly as they did in life. You have not joined them yet, you are still a shadow, an absence. It takes time, perhaps. You are still around? Unwilling to let go?

One old friend, perhaps the only true believer we know, says the dead are allowed to hang about for a while. Before (presumably) they report to St Peter. This to explain the puzzling appearance of the walking sticks I found in the umbrella stand when I finally got home from the hospital; both the right size for me, one with a spike for country walking, the other with a ferrule for London pavements. No one has admitted to putting them there, or to opening the door to someone who might have delivered them. The one with the spike for rough ground still had its price ticket on, though not its provenance: no shop from which to enquire the name of the purchaser. It's the sort of thing Dad would do, says our daughter.

Impossible, therefore, to know if you are aware of what happened. I will try to tell you, though not necessarily in exact chronological order: at the moment memories seem to leapfrog over each other. When I first thought of writing to you, some kind friends suggested it might be good therapy, others feared that it would distress me. I see it as a professional challenge, which I know you would understand. Think of it as a kind of crime story. Always, in latter years anyway, your favourite bedtime reading.

We had no foreboding. We were going to Cambridge to a party for John's eightieth birthday. There was to be a boat on the river, a cheerful evening of food and drink and old friends making merry. We had booked into what we had been assured was a good hotel close to the landing-stage, chosen the clothes to change into after a light lunch and a siesta, discussed whether you should take your new blue velvet jacket and decided it might be too warm. Which led to a reminiscence about a similar jacket you had once owned in the far-off days when we all smoked, a dark green velvet that a woman had burned a hole in when she was talking to you at some crowded occasion that we hadn't really wanted to attend. We agreed it was interesting, when we were both having memory difficulties with the names of close friends, that this woman's name and appearance was instantly recalled by us both even though we had not seen her since she brushed your expensive velvet sleeve with her lit cigarette all those years ago.

We took a taxi to King's Cross and rolled our overnight bag to the semi-derelict part of the station that trains to Cambridge and King's Lynn depart from, bought first-class tickets as a small indulgence, a fitting prelude to a party, and caught the twelve forty-five train. We were in plenty of time to settle ourselves into seats, take out our various newspapers, books, magazines, the *New Statesman*, the *Spectator*. We had spent the evening before discussing what we had organised for the months after the party in Cambridge: visiting Beate in Munich, eight weeks or so in Greece, working and swimming, a cruise to the Arctic, an autumn trip to see our New Zealand family. Perhaps we were both contemplating these future plans as we smiled at each other. Congratulating ourselves on successfully setting out on the first journey of a busy year?

That was the last time I saw you, the last thing I remember. I was in total blackness. There was the voice in the tunnel telling me you were dead, a little later there were a few scattered pictures that are still vivid in my mind. The most memorable and comforting image is one of our family, brother and sister-in-law, children, grandchildren, nieces, standing around me as I lay in some sort of cot bed, looking down at me like cherubs from a painted ceiling. I was happy to see them if a little puzzled to see the daughter from New Zealand among them. I wanted to ask you why you hadn't told me she was coming. I wondered why you were not with them.

Slowly, fretfully drifting in and out of consciousness, I began to understand. The train we had so confidently boarded had been speeding at almost a hundred miles an hour and the train had derailed. Someone, I can't remember who, showed me a newspaper photograph of the carriage we had been sitting in tilted on its side on a station platform next to a large notice that said WELCOME TO POTTERS BAR. And I heard someone from the company responsible for the upkeep of the track — the chairman, the chief executive? —

speak on the radio. As I remember it, he said that his "heart bled for the victims", and, at some other point, more surprisingly, that "the alignment of points was not in the maintenance contract".

That was the first I heard of points 2182A. I remember thinking at the time that it sounded odd. Surely, maintaining a railway line so that trains could run along it safely ought to include making sure that the points were functioning properly? I think I said so to someone, a shadowy person sitting beside me, who agreed that the privatisation of the railways, dividing the tracks and the trains and the signals among separate commercial companies had always been a recipe for disaster. I remember that I became briefly indignant about Mrs Thatcher — or Margaret Roberts, as I still thought of her from our student days together at Oxford, and my visitor reminded me that it was another Tory prime minister who had actually carried out the policy of dismantling the old British Rail and made a hash of it. I started to argue, I think, and then unpleasant twinges from my smashed skeleton — broken ribs, legs, arms, collar-bone — distracted me from political discussion and I pressed the kind little button that so reliably delivered relief from acute pain and a release from the moment into a warm, timeless cloudiness.

I know more now. I have become familiar with a number of excellent railway magazines and acquired several interesting pen-pals: retired railwaymen and sophisticated railway buffs, one of them a professor of classics, who write to me with varying degrees of restrained anger and technical knowledge. You were killed because we had taken our seats in the only first-class coach, which was the last coach of the train. Points 2182A, just south of Potters Bar, were set for running along the down fast line. The first two coaches ran normally but as the third coach reached the points the right-hand blade moved, derailing its rear bogie and our coach, the fourth. Teach us not to get above ourselves and buy first-class tickets, perhaps, but that is a lesson too late for you to learn.

The right-hand blade moved because the lock-stretcher bar at the front of the points snapped. It was the only bar holding the point blades together although it was not designed to do so. The blades should have been held together by two adjustable stretcher bars. But bolts were missing from one end of each stretcher bar, making them useless. The rear bogie of the fourth coach derailed with the right-hand switch blade closed, twisting the coach round until, moving almost sideways, it rolled on to the platform of the station and finally stopped, wedged under the platform canopies. And by then you were dead.

I know you were killed instantly, and didn't lie for hours tortured and twisted and screaming, because the man who saved my life told me so. You may think he lied to be kind, but he is not the sort of man to lie. He is in the Air Force, a squadron leader who looks a little like the heroes of our wartime youth, upright, fresh-faced, a model of the kind of goodness and decency that does not admit lying.

He was the only other person in our doomed first-class carriage, which in fact was no more than a few rows of dusty seats separated by a glass door from identical dusty seats in the rest of the coach. Like me, he was sitting with his back to the engine; you were facing it, opposite me. When the crash came, he says, he watched you rise from your seat just as he realised he was rising from his. He saw you flying towards him. I visualise this scene; for some reason in my clear mental picture you are flying stark naked, arms akimbo, thick grey hair streaming. Our squadron leader remembers throwing himself aside to avoid colliding with you in mid-air, and then — minutes later, seconds? — grasping the luggage rack.

Younger and stronger than either of us, he was able to save himself. I don't know how long it was before the firemen freed us from the mangled coach. There was nothing to be done for you, so our travel companion looked for me. I was trapped under the seat I had been sitting on and the table. He couldn't release me; he could see I was broken and bleeding. He made me as comfortable as he could and talked to me. He said I told him I didn't want to stay, I was in too much pain, but he was determined I should. He talked to me to keep me breathing. And my treacherous body — this temporary habitation — made its own perverse decision and conspired with him against me.

So I was alive when they took me to hospital. The squadron leader stayed with me until I was put in the ambulance. He knew my first name, that was all I had told him. Later, when he had been discharged after his cuts and bruises had been given attention, he tried to find out what had happened to me but no one would tell him. He wasn't a relation, they said.

You were missing for hours. I must have known you were missing because they tell me that I tried to get out of my bed in order to look for you and abused our poor son when he prevented me injuring myself further by attempting to stand on my broken legs. He says the local hospital was woefully understaffed — certainly not equipped to deal with the victims of a major train crash — and that he had difficulty in getting proper medical attention for me. This is only what I have been told, you understand. Our children were the ones who suffered all through that long night, waiting for you to be found, waiting for me to die. All I remember is a dream.

I was in a London gentleman's club — that was how I explained it to myself in my dream. It was arranged like a traditional theatre, rows of red velvet seats rising up and men in old-fashioned formal clothes seated upon them. All these men sat quite still, their eyes closed, as if dead or asleep, and steel bars fenced them in. There was a bar across my seat as well and unlike the comatose men I was struggling to climb over it, trying to escape, though why and from what I cannot remember. But you will know why I thought I would be able to find you. There was that time you slipped on a narrow stair when we were staying with friends in the country and dislocated your shoulder. The surgeon at the local hospital put it back for you, but when our host and I came to fetch you home for dinner, you were not to be found. The hospital denied all knowledge of you. While our friend argued with the management I searched the hospital and ran you to earth in a sluice, abandoned on a trolley and still dozy from the anaesthetic.

So that was why, in my toxic confusion, I fought to climb out of my bed in that hospital. You had toxic confusion once, that Christmas you had pneumonia. Wandering, not making sense, and then, when you finally arrived in the hospital, you said that the wall opposite your bed was moving, a moving picture of a rural scene, ladies and gentlemen in eighteenth-century costume preparing a picnic. A Watteau, you said, and the pretty nurses consoled you. "I expect we look strange too," one of them said. She was wearing a mask, because they feared you might have legionnaire's disease, and reindeer antlers on her head because it was Christmas Day.

In my hospital there was no talk of points 2182A for a while. Or if there was I have forgotten it. I was locked away, imprisoned by pain. How my visitors were feeling, what they were doing at my bedside, how far they had travelled to see me, what difficulties your death, my incapacity had made for them — if I was aware of these things at all, it was a blurred understanding, much-loved friends and family seen through fog, or a filmy gauze curtain. The nurses were more solid, more clearly etched; I suppose because I recognised their importance to my comfort. Like all NHS hospitals, this one was short of nurses but there

14

was one who was wonderful: when she was in the ward I felt safe as a child with her mother. It was her I missed when they took me away to a private hospital where there would be more physiotherapists to "get me back on my feet". I couldn't sit up in bed at this point, let alone get on my feet. I longed to be propped up on pillows but hadn't the strength to do it alone, and since lifting patients is apparently against hospital rules nowadays, in case nurses should hurt their backs, only the lovely staff nurse and a young male nurse were prepared to help me move up in the bed. I tell you this not asking for pity but to explain why, after the accident, I had not at once set about identifying the cause of your absence, which was still, for much of this time, mysterious to me. I was preoccupied with my own uncomfortable physical situation.

I had been bashed on the head and was interestingly bruised down one side of my face. I asked for a mirror out of curiosity as much as vanity, having been fascinated by the deep purple colour of my right arm, which was the only bit of my body I could properly see, the only limb that was not encased in white plaster. There were horrid pipes dangling from every orifice, disgusting but painless except for the oxygen tubes that scratched my nose. I was afraid to be left alone for an instant and wailed if they closed the curtains around me: one of the strongest emotions I can recall from that time is a terrified hatred of the material the curtains were made from, a particular floral pattern that seemed to be connected with some unpleasant event in the past that I couldn't (and still can't) identify. I thought that when you came you would remember it for me.

But of course you didn't come and I suppose, in part of my battered mind, I knew that you wouldn't, only choosing to cling to the illusion as a shield, a protection. Not faking it exactly, though since then I have retreated from time to time into a half-conscious role of "Potters Bar Victim", in order to avoid having to make a decision about some quite irrelevant matter.

I dislike the word "victim". I dislike being told that I "lost" my husband — as if I had idly abandoned you by the side of the railway track like an unwanted pair of old shoes. In spite of the excellent pills the psychiatrist has prescribed for me that take the sharp edge off emotions, misuse of language still fills me with an only just controllable rage. You were killed. I didn't lose you. And I am not a victim. I am an angry survivor.

And there are plenty like me. Some in better shape, some in worse. A pretty girl in a wheelchair came to my bedside in the first hospital; a young Australian who had recently arrived in England to work as a nurse here and travel in Europe. She had been thrown from the train and trapped under wreckage. She said, "When I woke up, I knew there was something wrong with my leg but I couldn't move it."

She was bleeding. She would have bled to death if one of the young men who happened to be at the station when the train derailed had not come to help her and make sure the paramedics knew she was alive. There were seven dead and seventy injured, thrown from their carriages like broken dolls and in some

16

cases, mine and the Australian nurse's among them, speed was important if they were to live. Until I spoke to the squadron leader and then, later, saw him speak on the documentary film that was made about the crash (a BBC Film of Record) I had been afraid that you had been among those abandoned as not obviously viable; disregarded, unnoticed.

The young men appeared in the film too, along with our daughter and the brave wife of the solicitor whose death had left her with four young children; the oldest, a handsome black girl of fourteen, spoke movingly and eloquently to the camera about the loss of her father. The young men spoke equally fluently about what they had seen, and it was clear that the memory of the chaos, the carnage, would haunt them for ever. And yet, months later, seeing them in the finished film, I found that I envied them because they had seen what had happened. This was why, I suppose, that the film did not disturb me as my family had feared that it would. I watched it without any sense of recognition. I had been unconscious, I remembered nothing, it was as if I had not been there.

Now, although my memory of the events in the weeks after the accident is still hazy, I can sometimes put them in some sort of order by pinning them down to the physical state I was in at the time and which hospital. There was better food at the private hospital and it was put within my reach. But I cannot be certain exactly when I heard a Snakehead speak for the first time. Or in which of his various Snakehead manifestations — rail executive, chairman of the contracting company, government spokesman — he did so. All these individuals said much the same thing, but the appearance of one might have suggested to me a name for the composite figure. All I can be sure of is that my ubiquitous Snakehead has smooth cropped hair and pale eyes, narrow-set on either side of a nose that is gently protuberant rather than craggy. And his voice is soft.

He said — and I am almost quite sure that this was in the first, National Health hospital, because the television I was watching, which our son had bought for me because there was a waiting list to rent one from the NHS, was to the right of my bed rather than a fixture high on the wall; that came later, included in the price of the room in the BUPA hospital I was taken to. Snakehead was being interviewed about the cause of the crash and, although naturally he expressed his deep and abiding sorrow for those killed and injured, he insisted that his company was not at fault in the matter of the missing bolts from the stretcher bars. He said, in his soft voice — which held a strangely regretful note on this occasion as if he genuinely, honestly, *truly* would have preferred to shoulder the blame himself — "It was sabotage. I have been shown compelling evidence."

It was risible even then. Saddam Hussein, Osama Bin Laden, or one of the other demons of our time surfacing in Potters Bar? The very name of the suburban station added to the absurdity.

The evidence that has been produced is not compelling, and I only mention it now because it was the first — *my* first, that is — real encounter with people whose overriding instinct is never to admit responsibility. I was naïve, of course. I suppose I am lucky to have lived so long believing that most men are for the most part honourable. And lucky to have taken up a profession in which owning up and telling the truth is rarely a financial disadvantage. But this personally fortunate situation leaves you unprepared. I think I assumed that what had happened was so obviously a national disaster that response from the railways and the government would be swift and helpful, people tumbling over each other to relieve and comfort the injured and those mourning their dead. Instead, apart from two "bereavement counsellors" who, so the children have told me, unexpectedly appeared in the middle of the night and seemed to be on the permanent staff of the railway or the construction company, the only public body to concern itself with the damaged survivors was the British Transport Police.

Would you have thought that? "Charlie's Angels", the children called them — is that a television series? One of those you and I never watched, no doubt thinking ourselves almighty superior. No, that's not fair. I watched — and still watch — news programmes, you preferred old cowboy films, snoozing in front of them in the early afternoon instead of taking a proper Greek siesta. Our Angels were — still are — two young women from a police unit that befriended families who had suffered some sort of unexpected and violent event, a fire, a crash, a murder. They were there from the beginning, advising, consoling, providing practical help with documents, death certificates and the like. Always at the other end of a telephone, always concerned and imaginative. When I was in the first hospital they came to see me bringing a pretty fruit bowl of red glass. They had guessed I might have too many flowers, which was true. The bowl sits at home now, on the dresser in our kitchen. It reminds me daily of the kindness of ordinary people.

Like the taxi driver who drove two of our friends from a main-line station to your memorial service in St Martin-in-the-Fields. It was a bright sunny day and as they came into Trafalgar Square the bells were ringing, a joyous sound in the clear London air. "Who's that for?" the taxi driver asked, and they told him it was for a friend who had been killed at Potters Bar. The driver shook his head and switched off his meter. "It's the least I can do," he said.

Ordinary people. What do I mean? I daresay corporation chairmen and executives — the Snakeheads of my story — have families, houses and gardens, human hopes and dreams like the rest of us. But what they do for a living is measured in money: own up to a fault, apologise, and the share price goes down.

I think, to begin with, none of us understood this.

TWO

The first time I met a Snakehead, I woke from my innocent slumber. I say "I" and not "we" because I think I was perhaps the only true innocent among the survivors; none of the others who attended this meeting with Snakehead had been injured and so shut away, as I had been, from the world. Although I had been out of hospital for a few months by this time, I still had a night nurse living with me as well as someone during the day: I became disorientated at night and needed help to get out of bed and go to the bathroom. I could stand, though, and walk with a stick, which was a small triumph; when I left the first hospital I couldn't sit up alone and was so afraid of falling off the bed that I had to have the rails securely pulled up on both sides all the time. Our New Zealand daughter came with me in the ambulance to the second hospital and held me safe on the stretcher, and when I finally got out of bed by myself a month later, our youngest daughter wept like a waterfall to see me standing alone. It was the first time I realised that they had all thought I was going to die.

I won't go on in this vein: continuing illness and inadequacy is as tedious to read about as it is to endure. But I want you to understand why I was not busy from the beginning organising protests in Trafalgar Square, or marching up Whitehall at the head of an outraged army with banners, demanding that your killers be brought to justice. I was too busy fighting for my own life.

Not consciously, you understand. I think if my situation had been presented clearly to me I would have made a different choice. I had never contemplated life without you; in fact, I think we had both unconsciously expected to die together. But presented with a physical challenge, my excellent constitution decided — entirely without my authority — not to take advantage of the opportunity offered by the inadequacies of the track-maintenance company.

When I came out of hospital to go to your funeral I was still in no shape for a battle. And from that day and the months that followed I now remember only some poignant milestones. Grandchildren singing bravely and beautifully both to the family in the crematorium chapel and later to the much larger audience at your memorial service; coming home and seeing for the first time your empty study, your mysteriously tidy desk; being given by the police the watch you were wearing at the time of the crash, the cheap waterproof watch I had bought you to wear for swimming in Greece even though I never understood why you wanted to know the time in the sea. I suppose those late wartime years in the Navy and in broadcasting afterwards. Both exact good time-keeping.

The watch is still working.

24

The first time I saw Snakehead was a different category of milestone. It was more of a wake-up call. We survivors and our families had several meetings before this one, with the Health and Safety Executive, with the police team in charge of the investigation, meetings that had alarmed me in prospect but turned out to be comfortably sympathetic in practice, conducted not by Snakeheads but by human beings who appeared as anxious as we were to discover what had gone so disastrously wrong. It was confronting Railtrack, the privatised company then in charge of the permanent way, that introduced me to my first clear example of Snakeheads and Snakish thinking.

I had been out of hospital for a couple of months. I wasn't yet angry. We met in an hotel in the Euston Road, in a smallish, fuggy room with three men from Railtrack sitting in front of us. I seem to remember they sat on a low platform but I cannot be certain, only that the chief Snakehead stood in the middle with two lesser Snakeheads at either side of him who never moved from their chairs. The one on Snakehead's left seemed to me to be wearing an arrogant, mildly contemptuous expression as if he wanted us to know that he had better things to do with his time.

Snakehead-in-chief made a short, moderately sympathetic introductory speech; on the surface a reasonable man with a difficult task, facing an audience of people whose sons and daughters, husbands and grandchildren had been killed in an avoidable accident. He shared our sorrow, he "knew how we must feel". But as he continued in this anodyne way I sensed a rustling, a nervous clearing of throats, a restiveness round me. One of our sons-in-law expressed this with a sharpness that did not feel quite appropriate at the time (though it did later) but succeeded in puncturing the balloon of politeness that seemed to be stifling us all, letting in a fresher air.

The newspapers had come out with a story about the compensation that was to be offered to the bereaved families. (I dislike the word "bereaved" as I do the word "victim" but I cannot think of a neater.) The story, offered in the article as fact, had said that a million pounds' compensation would be paid to each family and that twelve million pounds had been "set aside" for this purpose.

Although some of us had received interim payments, for nursing care, operations, funerals, and in our case to fly the New Zealand family to London, we knew that no such general compensatory offer had been made to anyone. But there had been three young Taiwanese women on the train, television journalists who were visiting and working in England and had ill-advisedly chosen that weekend to go sightseeing in Cambridge. Now one was in a coma in Beijing, and the families of the two girls who had died in the crash had been besieged in their own country by insolvent — or greedy — friends and relations who had seen the piece in the papers; it had added painfully to their agony and loss.

When this was reported to him, Snakehead apologised: it was a mistake, or perhaps a misunderstanding, by some junior person in the publicity department. And of course we all knew, didn't we, what the press were like? But he seemed genuinely astonished by the hurt and anger the "mistake" seemed to have caused. This was the moment when I began to doubt Snakehead's connection to the world of ordinary people.

Then the word "liability" was mentioned and instead of another apology we were treated to a fluent and well-rehearsed lecture on the difference between liability and responsibility. Snakehead felt humanly responsible, he insisted, because this unfortunate incident had occurred on his patch, but liability was a different matter. "Legal?" someone growled, from what I was beginning to think of as the back of the class. The rest of us sat meekly enough in our temporary schoolroom except for occasional, barely audible mutterings, which Snakehead was quick to sense if not to hear, pale eyes flickering from face to face, head cocked to one side, an alert teacher, on his feet and preparing for mutiny.

The mutterings began to grow louder. The solicitor's widow who had been left with four dependent children was the immediate focus. Several months later, in the documentary film, she was to speak movingly about her broken life and weep, but at this meeting she was silent, petrified, it seemed, with grief. Her brother who had hoped to fly to London as soon as the accident happened, had been refused a visa from the British Embassy in Nigeria. (Whether I knew this at the time or heard it later I cannot now remember. You would have remembered the detail. As it is, half our shared memory bank has died with you.) In the absence of this brother she was supported by a cousin, a youngish doctor practising in London, and Snakehead's professionally cool delivery had provoked him. He got to his feet and launched into a long and passionate speech on what it was like to tell four children, three of them too young to comprehend the finality of his message, that their beloved father was not coming back, that their happy family life was over for ever.

My eyes were misted by the time he ended. English was not the doctor's first language but his gallant fumbling with unfamiliar words made his statement all the more moving. Snakehead heard him out with a practised expression of respectful understanding and sorrow but the lesser Snakehead on his left seemed apparently unable to control his amusement. He then put his hand across his mouth, which made his behaviour even more insulting. I expected the senior Snakehead to rebuke him but he avoided looking in his underling's direction and that made me angry. I said to the offender, surprising myself by my fierce and peremptory tone, "What's so funny?"

He sat for the rest of the session looking uncomfortably solemn and silent. I was silent too for a while; embarrassed by my unexpected success. But the natural emotion with which the doctor had been able to talk about his cousin's predicament gave courage to some of those who had until then been too inhibited to speak. A woman whose student son had been killed, his lecture notes for his Ph.D. scattered over the rubble on the bank; daughters whose mother had died when the derailed train had smashed into the bridge she was walking beneath; a grandmother mourning the granddaughter she had brought up alone. What they — what we — were all needing to know was why this had happened, what was going to be done to stop it happening again, why had no one from the railway said they were sorry. Admitting liability would be a step in the right direction. An acknowledgement, at least.

"Legal," repeated the gruff male voice from the back of the class. "First, let's kill all the lawyers." Snakehead ignored this intrusion. He settled his gaze on those of us in the front rows and explained patiently. The police investigation was not yet complete. Nor had the Health and Safety Executive reported finally. The possibility that sabotage, or sophisticated vandalism by a resentful track worker, was responsible had not yet been ruled out. It would be premature to rush to conclusions.

"If you were a saboteur or a sophisticated vandal, would you do your dirty work within the security lights of the station?" someone asked.

Snakehead smiled indulgently and replied in what he presumably considered a suitably playful tone, saying that he couldn't really give an answer to that question as he had never considered becoming a professional saboteur. He was less amused when someone else pointed out that the HSE's first report had clearly said that although they had not found any evidence of sabotage they had found plenty of evidence of poor maintenance. He could only repeat that "we" had to be patient — as if we were all, casualties and Snakeheads, at one in this matter.

"Liability," said the voice from the back row. "Legal responsibility, that's what you're ducking."

Snakehead shook his head sadly. He could only tell us what he had said many times before: that compensation claims, if that was the concern, would be dealt with as if liability had been admitted. In answer to this there was some discreet tittering of disbelief that was quickly silenced, perhaps from general embarrassment. It is possible that the lying newspaper reports about the million-pound offers to the families of the dead had reminded us all of the popular — and often thoughtless — deriding of the "compensation culture" so that the idea that the cost of a death could be calculated had become somehow shameful. Demeaning. We had not yet understood the ways that the minds of Snakehead's lawyers were likely to work: had not yet realised that a child or an unemployed old person is worth nothing in law, since neither young nor old support anyone else, nor contribute to the economy. You might think from this that murdering someone in either of these socially useless categories could be a not unreasonable defence for a killer but there is no such logic in the workings of the law. The three daughters of the woman who was killed by rubble falling from the bridge have been told by Railtrack's lawyers (since this meeting) that they will receive no compensation for the gap their mother's death would leave in their lives. "As if her life was worthless," one of them said.

You would have thought that the value of a life was a matter for philosophers rather than lawyers. For the young — who knows? The death of a deaf baby could deprive the world of a Beethoven. A merciful pillow over the face could spare a hopelessly damaged child years of helpless misery. Indeed, it is arguable that a few of those who had died in the crash were luckier than some of the survivors: a girl in a coma, from which she may never wake or have any meaningful existence if she does; a young ballet dancer who will never walk again. Sometimes I tell myself that you, my love, have at least been spared the final indignities of old age, but I find no comfort in this admirably unselfish thought. If you had died coughing your lungs out when you had pneumonia that winter there would at least have been time to say goodbye, to ask where you had put the key to the drawer in the bureau that you always liked to keep locked for some reason.

What was it you were so anxious to hide — hide from whom, anyway? One of the children opened the drawer finally and there was nothing in it except some out-of-date passports and four premium-bond certificates for ten pounds apiece. Not much to interest a burglar; nothing even, disappointingly, to shed light on some hitherto unknown family scandal. Why were you such a squirrel?

All those years of communal living, at boarding-school and then in the Navy? Needing somewhere to hide old letters, anything you wanted kept private? Or at home, conceal from your parents?

How little I know about you. How little we knew about each other. Or so it seems sometimes when there is something relatively simple I want to ask you.

＊　＊　＊

After the meeting with Snakehead, our battling solicitor took us all for a drink in the hotel bar, which turned out surprisingly jolly. That is, the jollity surprised me at the time. Now it seems obvious: shared experience had introduced us; there was no need for the stock questioning, the usual circling and sniffing around in order to get acquainted. Of course we asked the same questions but "Where do you live?" had a different and more poignant purpose now. Where was your child, your husband, your parent going? Why were they on that particular train?

I have seen the film that the railway security cameras took of the platform and the passengers and the train before it drew away. You and I had not been in a hurry. As usual, owing to my travel neurosis, we had arrived almost in time to catch the earlier train. That we were not quite early enough was because of the success you have had over the years in persuading me that it is not absolutely necessary to camp overnight at the airport or the railway station from which the plane or train you intend to catch is leaving the following morning.

So on the film we were walking at a leisurely pace to our doom. I was wheeling the small overnight suitcase, you were carrying your chosen jacket in its suit cover. Others, among them the Nigerian solicitor who had run, briefcase swinging, to leap into a carriage at the very last minute, almost missed the train. Had he been hurrying home to his family? Curiously, that grey, blurred video, which I have seen only once, affected me more painfully than the skilled documentary that was made later, or, indeed, than anything I have been told about the crash. It was the innocence of those jerkily moving, almost transparent figures, so unaware of what lay ahead of them, that twisted my gut and made me want to shout, *Stop, you fools! Get a later train!*

In fact, the Nigerian had an afternoon appointment with an asylum-seeker in Cambridge. The Ph.D. student was going home to his mother; the young woman to see her grandmother. And we, of course, were going to a party. Catching this unnecessarily early train.

While we were drinking together after the meeting none of us had yet seen the railway video; it was sent later by the ever-helpful police, is my recollection. The conversation in the bar was friendly, not intimate but there was a basic feeling of intimacy all the same, as if we were a widely dispersed family who were conscious of a bond even though we met very rarely. I think that most of us shared an element of shocked disappointment at the lack of understanding that had been shown by the trio of Snakeheads. It was something we had not encountered from the police, or from the Health and Safety Executive, and all the newspaper reports and television discussions had been generally sympathetic towards we "victims", if sometimes keener on publicising dramatic personal stories than arguments about the cause of the crash.

To my surprise (and mild irritation) no one except me seemed to be interested in discussing the general failures of privatisation. I looked for the man with the growly voice, thinking he might be a useful ally, but since I didn't know what he looked like and he hadn't spoken, I assumed he had given up and gone home.

I suppose, without realising it, I was already moving into crusader mode. I had been sent a copy of a definitive lecture given by a superb railway buff (the professor of classics) and it had fired me into a fine indignation: you had been killed by the lamentable failure of all governments since 1945 to take proper responsibility for the country's rail infrastructure and I was going to do what I could to put that negligence right. I had been encouraged in this hubristic intention by various radio and television programmes on which I had been invited to appear and broadcast my opinions without contradiction. An element of agreeable self-flattery in this, as you would rightly say, but it may do some good eventually and has been distracting for me, keeping me balanced on the edge of the Slough of Despond.

There was one man in the bar who gave me hope of a rousing political discussion when he said he was only interested in railway safety, but it turned out that this was merely the prelude to a self-satisfied announcement that he was totally uninterested in receiving any money, that the only "compensation" he wanted was an assurance that the kind of accident that had killed our "loved ones" would not happen again.

This unexceptionable statement brought only a very brief silence before someone pointed out mildly that there might possibly be a few people for whom money was vital; perhaps, since her predicament was the most obvious, thinking of the solicitor's widow and her young family. She would have sprung to my mind anyway. But I realised I had not thought about "payment for your death" because I had assumed that "compensation" meant something different from necessary income for widows and orphans. Rather a kind of apology. As if to say, "Of course we can't recompense you for your dead child, your dead husband or wife, please forgive us, but this is the best we can do."

Unfortunately (and naturally, as no doubt you will recall) this kind of conversation brought out, as it always does, the worst in me. The frivolous, anyway. I said, heard myself saying, "I don't really see why they shouldn't pay out, give some of us who don't need it the money for an expensive cruise. Or buying a new dress, or whatever takes our fancy."

There was, as you might expect and as I deserved, an embarrassed pause. Luckily, luckily for me, anyway, the gruff-voiced male had been with us all this time, an inconspicuous ginger-haired figure sitting, as I now saw, to the left but a fraction behind the gentleman who was too grand to expect compensation because he wanted the heavens to move and the railways miraculously made as safe and speedy as the French railway system.

(Remember, after your father died and we went by rail to visit his bankers in Berne? When we were about to go home, you realised that our return entailed changing trains at Lausanne with only ten minutes to spare so you asked the receptionist if we should perhaps catch an earlier train.

He said, "But you have ten minutes. It will present no difficulty."

You said, patiently, "The train from Berne might be late," and he looked puzzled. He said, "Late?" as if the sound as well as the concept presented a difficulty. "Our trains are never late."

And of course it wasn't. Both trains, clean, comfortable and reliable, lulled us into a false sense of security: by the time Eurostar arrived at Waterloo we were amazed to find London in its usual traffic chaos.)

Gruff-voice said, "You'll have a fight on your hands if you want them to pay. We've got to make them admit liability."

I woke up yesterday morning with a brilliant idea. I would ring you on your mobile number. I suppose I'd had a dream. A few minutes later my confidence that you would answer diminished but the idea lingered, a little shame-faced, at the back of my mind. I got up, dressed, had breakfast, went to my desk. I thought I had put both our mobile numbers at the front of last year's diary. I found the diary but the numbers were absent. I restrained myself from examining other diaries and sat down to work. Our daughter came, as she does most days. We had lunch. After a glass of wine I confessed my folly. She said, "I've already done that, several months ago. There is no one there."

THREE

In spite of a temporary relief that Gruff-voice was still with us, I was not convinced that his point about liability was of such overwhelming importance. Although my original veil of innocence was growing more than a little threadbare, I could not entirely abandon my belief that after such a disaster relief would follow eventually. Cautious bureaucracy in the Snakehead railway companies was for the moment impeding delivery, but seven dead and seventy injured, some of them terribly, was something that the government could not afford to ignore. Even Louise could not persuade me that we had a real fight on our hands until a year after the crash that took you away from us.

But before I tell you about the anniversary ceremony, I must acquaint you with our doughty solicitor.

The children told me they had heard about her from the pretty Australian with the broken leg and, along with my brother, had come to the conclusion that you would have approved of her. (Or that was one of the explanations: all I can be sure of is that she was there when I first became aware of the world around me although I cannot recall the exact moment that was.)

She works on what the Americans call a no-win-no-fee basis, which in England we call, more ambiguously and decorously, a conditional fee. This means that there must be an element of assessment on her part before she takes on a cause, and occasional rejection of one that is obviously lost from the beginning, but I saw her as I still see her, and I think correctly, as a gallant heroine, fighting for helpless ordinary people against the faceless organisations that usually defeat them. The power of the corporations is only the power of money. Although some of us would have qualified for help from the government on financial grounds, we were refused it. The original scheme, set up by the Attlee government after the Second World War to make legal provision for everyone, has been so eroded by governments anxious to save money that only the very rich can afford justice now. The only access for most of us is through firms that will work for a conditional fee.

Did you know that the right to legal aid for physical injury no longer exists? It was removed by the Labour government that you and I worked and voted for all our adult lives. Naturally, they said at the time that if there was a major disaster this restriction would not apply, but our solicitor's request to the Legal Services Commission for funding so that we could take Railtrack to the High Court to make them admit liability was turned down: our railway crash was not, apparently, a "matter of public interest".

More on that later. (Louise is still working on it.) The only thing you need to know for the moment is that the family were right: you would have been delighted to know she was looking after us all. Determined, ambitious, lovely to look at, sparkling with intelligence. Younger than you and me, but not too young, and above all, a fighter. A sexy fighter. You would have enjoyed flirting with her at a dinner table. And I believe she is genuinely concerned for us all.

I cannot remember what she had to do with the anniversary ceremony. (There are some advantages in my lapses of memory: they mean that I only recall the important things. Or so I tell myself anyway.) But I believe that it was mostly organised by the people of Potters Bar.

As I write that sentence I realise that this is the first time that I have really acknowledged how much their lives must have been affected by the crash and not only the local rescue services, police and firemen, bystanders, doctors and nurses, but the whole of the town's population since roads and schools were closed and hospitals crowded. A young man who happened to be at the station said that the one thing he would never forget was the silence that came after the metallic screams of the carriage ripping into the station platform and roof. "That was the scary part. It was just silence. It was just silence. Really eerie. Kind of haunting." The only sound was the swinging sign saying WELCOME TO POTTERS BAR, "like in a deserted town in an old western movie".

He said that the "sound of the silence" would stay with him all his life.

As what he said will stay with me.

We drove to Potters Bar. There was no public lavatory on the platform and as we hurried through the subway to a pub on the other side of the station trains rattled and clattered above us.

It was a blustery, cold day, and in the warmth of the pub we took our time over a glass of wine and a bowl of soup before we went to the memorial garden beside the station that was to be dedicated to the memory of the dead.

There had been a Buddhist ceremony already. As our group nodded and smiled and greeted each other, I saw the Taiwanese families for the first time and remembered the girls who had been setting out for a happy holiday weekend in Cambridge. Two had been killed, one was still in a coma in hospital in Beijing. I wondered if their families had known each other before the crash or if, like the rest of us, they had only met afterwards, strangers thrown together by malicious chance.

An *ad hoc*, accidental family.

There was no sign of Gruff-voice but once I thought about it I decided that I should not have expected to see him. I told myself that I should have guessed by the sound of him and a brief glimpse of his gingery scowl that this kind of occasion was not to his taste. It was not to mine, either, but as you know, I often do things I am expected to do even though I don't want to: I would like to think this shows politeness and concern for other people but it may simply be lack of self-confidence. Lack of what your father would have called *backbone*.

Though in this case I had no choice. Most of our family were there. I could have feigned illness. But I would not have liked to confess the truth: that I was terrified of *not feeling anything*. You would have understood that but pointed out that it didn't matter because it wouldn't *show*.

And I hope that it didn't. The local vicar spoke appropriate words. Music was played, flowers were laid. I had not thought to bring any and should have been mortified by this failure but was not. The youngest grandson brought blossom from the tree he had planted for you, a cherry that will bloom every May. The month of the crash — and your death. A granddaughter brought some flowers for me in case the press should want a touching picture of me laying them under the grey sky. The police were there in full regalia. The squadron leader was there, with his wife. Our son's oldest boy had picked a bunch of flowers from the garden to match a card on which he had written those lovely lines from *Hamlet* when Ophelia is mourning her father: "*There's rosemary, that's for remembrance; pray you, love, remember. And there is pansies, that's for thoughts . . .*"

You know the rest.

I should have wept. All around me people were wiping their eyes. I was ashamed to be so unmoved by this moving occasion. Then I looked at the Nigerian solicitor's family. All the children were beautifully dressed in what were clearly spanking new clothes: gleaming shoes, blazers, ties for the boys, hats for the girls, knee-length white socks . . .

And suddenly I was crying, or at least watery-eyed. It was the children's clothes, especially bought for this ceremony. I thought it was all, perhaps, that the three younger ones would remember about their dead father. *I had a pair of new shoes and new socks and a hat . . .*

The press were there, as they seemed always to be, taking pictures and films of the sad flowers and dismal skies and holding microphones near anyone who looked good for a few weepy quotes. I think we had all learned to find this interest useful: the press have been stalwart supporters of our fight for justice and a public inquiry. So we were prepared to crowd into a room in a youth club round the corner from the station and to answer questions.

I sat at the front with the squadron leader, a mother whose son had been killed, and the Taiwanese families. It was an unsuitably small room and airlessly hot. The usual questions were asked, the usual answers were given. No, there had been no response from Railtrack or Jarvis. No admission of liability, no apology, no intervention from the Minister for Transport. The combination of heat and familiarity began to produce yawning and torpor.

It was the Taiwanese who woke up the meeting. Two of the women spoke, reading from prepared statements in their own language, their voices breaking. Everyone listened uncomprehendingly but respectfully. Then a young man, a son, or a nephew, stood and translated what they had said. His English was faltering but the message was clear. "With a bright future full of potential, our vibrant, happy daughters travelled to your country full of hope but they were returned to us as ash. We thought Britain was a cultured and civilised and democratic country where human rights were fully respected and social justice upheld. We have been proved wrong."

A year after the crash and they had still heard nothing from Britain, nothing from the government or the rail companies; the ashes of their daughters had been returned in an unmarked box. There had been no letter with the ashes, no word of commiseration or explanation. None of the rest of us had heard anything either, but suddenly, the fact that these strangers from the other side of the world had been treated in the same dismissive way filled me with a particularly acute shame and sorrow.

And I was not alone. When the young man had finished and sat down, no one spoke. For what seemed several minutes, the only sound in the room was the soft weeping of the Taiwanese women. Then a throat was cleared at the back of the room and a voice that I recognised said, "I apologise for my country."

Gruff-voice was here after all.

I cannot remember leaving the room. I do remember seeing a line of waiting coaches through a mist of tears and wondering for a confused moment, as I climbed into the last one, where I was to be taken now, what new ordeal faced us all. Then I saw that some of our group had been delayed by the press, our daughter among them, talking to Sky Television. After a moment of freezing panic when the other coaches began to move off, I understood with relief that mine was staying behind to pick up the stragglers.

I am so afraid of being left alone, abandoned, it makes me stupid and helpless.

My coach waited around forty minutes. By the time we arrived at our destination we had missed lunch and were taken on a windy walk to a large marquee that had been set up in the grounds of a school for the next part of the ceremony. The order of the events that followed is vague in my mind; I suppose I was cold and hungry and suffering from withheld — or denied — emotion. There was a local jazz band, a local amateur opera singer and a few numbers played by the school band that had (so I learned later) been deprived of its guitarist because thieves had stolen the guitar while everyone was at the memorial garden. After the short service with hymns and readings a candle was lit for each family; our youngest grandson lit yours. I remember the golden light from the candles and the family members silhouetted darkly against it, and the sudden painful lump in my throat.

Why should candlelight produce this predictably sentimental response in someone as temporarily wooden as me? Not that it matters. At least — so I comforted myself in that moment — it showed that I was not totally deficient in proper feelings. But immediately afterwards all that I wanted was to get away, to warm my frozen fingers, to order a large glass of wine and something to eat. Tea was to be provided in the marquee but I encouraged the family to leave as soon as they could do so politely and meet up in the nearest warm public house.

I can't remember exactly who joined us — I remember Jane Sayers of Films of Record who made the good documentary about the accident, the squadron leader and his wife as well as our family — but we were all glad to be out of the cold and I was not the only one who was inclined to giggle with relief that it was all over. It wasn't until we were driving back to London that I began to be angry.

When I think about it now I am astonished that it had taken me so long to understand that Gruff-voice was right. It wasn't only the children dressed in their new and beautiful clothes and the movingly expressed grief of the Taiwanese mothers that brought me to this belated conclusion but an *absence*. I had seen the British Transport Police, smart in their best uniforms, laying flowers, men from the Health and Safety Executive, the lawyers, the bereaved and injured families, a scattering of local people, but I had not seen anyone from the railways, and although our daughter says that she is sure a representative was there, I have decided that this was a purely charitable assumption on her part. She would no doubt argue that it would be indelicate of those responsible for killing and maiming so many people to make themselves known to their victims on such a painful occasion. I may, I admit, be wrong and simply using an argument that suits me. All I can be sure of is that I saw no one I recognised as a railwayman at the memorial garden; certainly not

Snakehead, or one of his minions. And it brought home to me what had clearly been obvious to everyone else from the beginning: that they were not prepared to admit their guilt, take responsibility for the dead and the injured.

To make them do so, we would have to fight.

I suppose I had been fighting already, I had just not acknowledged the nature of the battle I was engaged in, the nature of the enemy. Taking part in a radio programme, appearing on television, writing a piece for a newspaper, I had seen my role as educational: I was simply explaining the situation we survivors found ourselves in through no fault of our own. When we had bought our tickets for this railway journey, we had expected a safe arrival, not an earthquake, smashing lives into pieces. I wanted people who had never experienced a catastrophe of this sort to know what it was like; if we could make sure our plight was properly understood, something would be done to help us.

After the anniversary, I knew it would not be so easy.

We had made such plans for that summer, do you remember? Among them was a cruise to the Arctic in August; a sentimental journey in memory of my father. Since he had been an engineer commander on an armed merchant cruiser during the war and you had also been in the Navy, if only as a young midshipman at the end of the war, sometimes, late in the evenings, he would bring out the whisky and talk about life at sea. His ship had been on North Sea Patrol and his favourite reminiscence was about the Shetland Bus, the name for the fleet of small fishing vessels that ran the gauntlet of the German submarines and battleships around the North Cape to take radio equipment and weapons to the Norwegian resistance. As you know, he was a bit of a romantic, my father, and after a good glass of whisky the gallantry of the fishermen who sailed those little boats often made him wipe a tear from his eyes before he heaved himself up from his chair (with some difficulty by the time he was in his ninetieth year) to refill the glasses.

We had already booked our tickets on this Swan-Hellenic cruise before the accident. Our daughter had cancelled them while I was still in the hospital, but I found the brochure in the travel drawer later on the next spring and the memory of the time when my father and mother were still alive, the children still young enough to enjoy spending holidays in their house by the sea, was so vivid suddenly, I could *feel* myself in my much younger skin. Only for a second or so, and it wasn't an altogether agreeable experience. (I felt *lumpy* — was I fatter then?)

I put the brochure back in the drawer — out of sight but not out of mind. I brooded over all the other things we had intended to do and now never would. Or, at least, not together. And thought, Why not? A way of keeping you with me? Surely nothing so silly . . .

I talked to our friend Phoebe about my sentimental impulse and she agreed to come with me. Both of us had the same reservations about the *idea* of a cruise:

retired couples, bald men in sports jackets, women in cardigans . . .

No. I won't wander off down that side alley. The holiday habits of middle-aged English people are nothing to do with this story. All I will tell you is that I had looked forward to being on a ship, cut off from the news, out of touch with my own anger and frustration. Impatient as always, I suppose I had secretly expected the enemy's defences to crumble at the first blast of a trumpet! So I was sitting on a burning sense of injustice — a bit like bad indigestion — and I was prescribing the cruise for myself as you would have prescribed a tablet of Gaviscon. And it is true that I felt better for it. Phoebe was a good companion and we laughed a lot together; the crenellated coast of Norway was theatrically beautiful; the reindeer unexpectedly small and velvety. You and my father were with me as I tramped — or limped would be more exact since my left ankle still refuses to heal — across the haunting wastes of the treeless North Cape. Not at my side, alas, but sitting by the fire in Herne Bay, both smoking your pipes as you sipped the whisky and talked sailors' talk, while my mother dozed in her chair and I drank the one glass my father thought proper for a young woman. I realise, when I remember your pipe, that this was a long time ago.

And I remember how loving you always were to my parents.

What this fortnight at sea accomplished for me was to firm up my resolution. I fantasised about what I would do if one of the Snakeheads — from the railways, either from Railtrack or from the privatised company charged with the maintenance of the track — had been among the other passengers. One evening we might meet and I would say . . .

What I would say to this as yet unidentified man defeated me. (There were no female Snakeheads in my fantasies, nor had there been any woman in the various meetings I had attended.) Walking on the deck after dark I imagined coming across him alone, pushing him over the rail into the sea, watching him struggle, terrified, before I called for help, threw him a lifebelt.

I disapprove of capital punishment, as you know. And there was no one on board the ship I could identify as a Snakehead. They were all pleasant, middle-aged men, happily coupled with pleasant, middle-aged wives; no act of my imagination could turn them into the cold-eyed corporate monsters who were denying us justice.

"You could go to the High Court," one of these pleasant men said one evening. "Get a summary judgement on liability." (I *promise* you I had not been spending evenings in the bar playing the ancient mariner. This evening was absolutely the only time I had talked about the accident to strangers. I had probably drunk too many glasses of wine; the man had sympathetic brown eyes, and his wife was a lawyer.)

I explained about the lack of legal aid and my own lack of money. We had a strong case but things can always go wrong. I almost said, *a mad judge*, but the woman was either a barrister or a solicitor, even a judge, and might feel she should defend her profession.

So I merely explained that taking the case to the High Court would be covered by the conditional-fee arrangement but should I do so on my own account and lose, I would be liable for Snakehead's costs, which could be enormous. (Our daughter thinks I am pusillanimous. I could sell my house. She would sell her house. Our shivering in the gutter wouldn't bring you back, I tell her. What would you do?)

"Apply to the LSC again," the woman lawyer said, adding kindly, in case I had not understood what the letters stood for, "the Legal Services Commission. No harm in a bit of persistence."

Her husband said, "Public bodies sometimes get to act like private corporations. The longer they spin things out the better for them, the less likely they'll have to pay out."

His wife looked at him with the faintest twitch of an eyebrow and he cleared his throat and glanced at his watch.

I said, "I do believe our solicitor has already decided to do that." And, stretching in my seat, grimacing slightly in order not-so-subtly to remind them of my tortured bones, "I'm so sorry, I think I've stayed up too long. And kept you talking. But it's been such a lovely evening."

The husband smiled at me — a trifle ruefully? With a touch of regret? I like to think he would have liked to spend longer in my company. A comforting weakness on my part? Probably. And he was perhaps a secret Snakehead himself.

After they had gone, I ordered a Metaxa for myself and a lemonade for Phoebe.

By the time the cruise was over the campaign had crept forward: I came home to the realisation that we were moving slowly towards the High Court. You will understand my reluctance to go for summary judgement on my own account without the protection of the conditional-fee arrangement. It was possible the railways and their sub-contractors, who were responsible for maintaining what we now know as the "permanent way" (the title of David Hare's splendid new play about the railways), would crumble and admit liability the moment they knew they were to be tested in court. On the other hand it was equally likely that, after the unfriendly press coverage they had already received since the accident, they would decide they had nothing to lose by defending themselves. They had admitted being at fault a few months ago, a while after "our" accident, when a train was derailed on the main line from King's Cross but on that occasion a piece of rail that should have been replaced the night before was actually missing, and a failure of maintenance was the only conclusion.

The circumstances in which points 2182A had failed were less clear. They were points of a kind that had been the subject of a safety leaflet published by Railtrack a year before the crash, which warned that they were difficult to adjust for trains at high speed. The bolts that should have secured points 2182A had been left lying by the side of the track. This was the "compelling" evidence of sabotage that the Snakehead from the maintenance company had spoken of publicly, on television, after the accident. Having presumably decided that Osama Bin Laden was unlikely to be the culprit on this occasion, his suggestion was that a "disgruntled employee" had deliberately neglected to replace them.

I went to meet the barrister who will represent us if and when we go to the High Court. Louise was there to introduce me and our son. The barrister is charming, clever and, I am quite sure, trustworthy. He understood my fears about landing up in the gutter if we were to lose the case and assured me that he would try to get the costs "capped" and that he would hope that a reasonable judge would agree. Louise had brought with her the photographs of the bolts that had been lying beside the line — either the Health and Safety Executive or the police had passed them on to her.

We sat and stared at these grey and black photographs; all four of us, so it seemed to me, hoping in a baffled way that some kind of explanation would leap out at us. I think I said something like, "Well, none of us is an engineer."

"Ancient Greece," the barrister murmured improbably. And then, even more strangely, "Do you see?"

See what? Mycaenae? Epidaurus? Tiryns — the site within walking distance of Nauplion? The places we both loved, although you loved them first, falling into what was to be a lifelong affair of the heart with Greece and the Greeks when you were working with the World Service, and Greece and Turkey were the countries you loved most. And by the time you retired, and we found our house in Nauplion, you had infected me with your passion and I was as eager to buy this tumbledown house as you were.

Would you have understood what the barrister was talking about? Neither our son nor Louise seemed surprised by the sudden lunacy that had seized this apparently sensible man, who continued, "We will need a good expert, someone who will stand up well in court."

I said nervously, "Ancient Greece?"

"Absolutely clogged with it," our son said.

"Impossible to screw the nut on without leaving a mark and there isn't one far enough up the bolt," the barrister said, looking at me, kindly explaining, I realised, that old packed-up grease was what they were talking about. Whether he had really understood how temporarily confused I had been I don't know but he went on, speaking slowly and carefully, as if to a backward child, "When you screw a nut to a bolt there is a tight fit down the thread. If they — or he — had tried to screw the bolt on properly there would have been a mark left on the grease all the way up the thread. And there isn't."

"Ah," I said. "Yes, I see."

"That insurance you've got," our son said. "Will that pay for an expert?"

The insurance is not, I think, one you would have known about. Our sharp-eyed children, who went through our papers after the accident, had read the small print. You had bought our off-peak, senior-citizen tickets with a credit card that paid out generously on injury or death. Our house insurance had a free legal cover with it. And, amazingly, when told what had happened, they offered fifty thousand pounds towards any legal costs that might arise, an unusual magnanimity from an insurance company. I would have expected it to have a more Snakish nature. It would not be enough money to pay the other side's costs should we lose in the High Court, but it was enough to pay for an expert in ancient grease.

The magnolia is out in the garden, buds trembling in the cold March wind. You dug your father's ashes around its roots, remember? Yours we intend to take to Greece this Easter. Against some law — bound to be: there is so much extra security since the war. Perhaps if disguised in an innocent container — for talcum powder, for example? Do they have sniffer dogs inspecting baggage for illegal ashes? Where would you like them scattered, anyway? Up on the castle?

Of course, I forgot, you don't know about the Iraq war. I remember that you went to the Albert Hall to demonstrate against the Suez disaster. And that I would have gone with you if I hadn't been pregnant.

What would you have thought about Iraq? The two adventures have some similarities but more differences: we were allies of the French in Suez and the Americans were against us. Would you have been part of the enormous crowd that marched against the war in Iraq as our middle daughter and your granddaughters were? As I would have been had my ankle allowed me to walk that sort of distance. What would you have said, what would you have done? Would you have walked with them?

I wish you would answer me.

FOUR

I miss you. All the time — not only when I cannot reach something off a high shelf, or need to fix the video-recorder, although of course there are many different occasions when I need your help for a specific reason that has nothing to do with our respective heights. As during some of the meetings we have had, with the police, with the Health and Safety Executive. I always realise after the meeting that there is a question I should have asked, something that you, whom I remember as being clearer-headed than me, or at least, after your years in the BBC more used to persuading, manipulating, would not have let slip. I am never sure what that question should have been, I am simply in the grip of a fierce frustration: I am sure that what you would have found out, made them tell you, is something pitifully obvious as well as important, but although it is hovering tantalisingly close, it is still just beyond the grasp of my mind. It makes me want to get angry, which I have always found unhelpful.

You lost your temper successfully once — that day we went to Bow Street police station with an order of release for our older son who had been arrested for possession of cannabis and sent to prison on remand. We had been to the High Court to get the order from a judge in chambers and reached Bow Street by noon. There was an old lady there, also waiting with an order, to get her husband out of prison, and the young policeman behind the counter told the three of us that we would have to wait a couple of hours for the "duty officer" to return from lunch and unlock the bail register. You said, mildly, that the duty officer was taking a long lunch-hour, wasn't he?, and the young policeman shrugged, a touch contemptuously. We all waited. After about half an hour, the old lady stubbed out her cigarette with a worn slipper and said something like, "They're all playing cards down the basement. It's the time gets you down. The hours you spend waiting." And you sat for a moment, clenching and unclenching your fists, before you jumped up, marched to the counter, thumped with both fists and shouted phrases like "insulting contempt for the public, petty bureaucracy, the sort of thing you might find in a police state . . ." And, of course, it worked. The young policeman picked up the telephone. When he put it down he said, "The officer is coming now, sir."

You were ashamed of your triumph afterwards, as I remember — though chiefly because when the duty officer came he attended to us before he even looked at the old lady. Although I have sometimes felt anger stirring during the meetings I have attended, it is not because anyone like that idle young policeman has occasioned it. These meetings are intended to be informative, reassuring, and for the most part they are.

The people conducting them are decent men, evidently conscious of working in the public interest. There is to be a gathering soon that, for various boring reasons, I cannot attend. So the policeman in charge of the investigation and someone from the HSE is going to visit me at home a few days later "to bring me up to date". The man from the HSE is making a special journey from Manchester.

I scent something sinister in this kind conscientiousness. Is it this that makes me angry? Our son and daughters are going to the earlier meeting and will be able to tell me what was said but I fear the police want to explain to me personally why they are not going to prosecute the railway company. I suspect the Crown Prosecution Service demands cast-iron evidence before it presents a case, and although any reasonable person would come to the conclusion that inadequate maintenance of points 2182A caused the crash, the unmarked ancient grease on the screws may not be enough to persuade cautious bureaucrats to "waste taxpayers' money" trying to prove it in court.

Still, we shall see. Watch this space.

Meanwhile there is just a possibility that a government minister may be willing to help us. Not as you might expect the Minister for Transport, who has shown zero interest in our predicament, but the Minister for Constitutional Affairs. Louise arranged an audience with him at the House of Commons. A sympathetic MP is to accompany us but Louise is not invited. It is all right, apparently, for members of the government or representatives of large corporations to have their legal advisers with them but ordinary people, who I am beginning to see as a quite separate and inferior species of being, are denied this privileged protection.

Our daughter was at this meeting, and the three daughters of the woman who was killed by falling bricks when the train crashed into the bridge above the railway line and was too old, so the lawyers acting for the railway have already told her family, for them to be entitled to compensation.

We met in the bone-chilly lobby of the Commons. The weather had suddenly turned bitter and the heating in the Houses of Parliament had failed. According to the helpful MP who was to be our guide and guardian on this occasion, the only warmth in the whole of the building was on the Conservative benches in the Chamber; the unfortunates on the government benches froze. As we did in the lobby. Foolishly, I had dressed to impress the minister in a new red trouser suit that I had bought for the spring, and I was not carrying an overcoat because it would have spoiled the effect.

You would have thought, wouldn't you, that after what had happened to us both I would have abandoned such trivial vanities? (Though you were always a natty dresser yourself: at your memorial service our son brought yellow roses for us all to wear as a reminder to everyone that for most of the year you were rarely abroad without a rose in your button-hole.)

On this occasion I had plenty of time to repent my lack of warm clothing. The lobby was busy: Parliament was debating a report on a matter that was the focus of current political excitement and the Chamber was unusually full. Well-known politicians were out in force, either welcoming or evading the press in the lobby. There was Robin Cook, waiting for his secretary to bring his raincoat and help him on with it, and I wondered if you would see him as I see him, as a hero. He was the only member of the government to resign in protest against the internationally illegal war in Iraq. He made a splendid resignation speech and continues to speak and behave in a dignified and exemplary manner. I cannot remember what you used to think of Robin Cook — *why* don't I remember? — although I think you would approve of his principled behaviour now, whatever you thought of him in the past.

I am more confident of your reaction to the report that was occupying everyone's attention on this particular day. Lord Hutton, a retired judge, had been asked to investigate a complicated sequence of events that included a government scandal, the suicide of a senior scientist, and an unfortunately phrased, though basically correct, news bulletin put out by the BBC. The bulletin was about the intelligence dossier that had been the declared reason for the Iraq war and the claim that it had been "sexed up" at the behest of Downing Street. The government had objected, as you would have expected, and appointed Lord Hutton, a conventional and establishment judge, to lead an inquiry. Today he was delivering his verdict to the Commons. I know it is a subject that would have involved you passionately and — in so far as the BBC was rapped over the knuckles and the government exonerated, leading to the resignation of the director general, the chairman of the governors and the journalist who had prepared the disputed report, while not one politician was honest enough to accept any responsibility — it certainly made me spit blood, but the only connection it has with this story is that it meant the minister was late.

By the time an aide had come to collect us we had been joined by two other shivering "victims", a youngish man and his wife. The man had been driving a truck under the bridge when the train crashed into it. He had not been badly hurt but he had spent hours helping to drag the dead and injured out of the wreckage and was so traumatised by this terrible experience that he lost his job and has been told he is unlikely to work again. He and his wife have three young children and at the time of this visit to the Commons they had received only two interim payments from Railtrack and were afraid for the future.

The wife told me this while we were waiting in the lobby. She is a strong, sparky girl, and she needs to be. The effect of the accident has been almost to deprive her husband of speech. He told me when we were introduced by our guardian MP that he "wasn't much good with words", and looked helplessly at his wife. And although once or twice later he answered a direct question, he could speak only in staccato spurts and with a desperate glance at her for assistance.

Eventually, we were taken into a room, mercifully supplied with an electric heater, and settled at one end of a long table. We were joined by a couple of men from the Legal Services Commission, the body who had earlier denied us legal aid because the safety of the railways was, in their view, not a matter of public interest. They looked at our suppliant group with what seemed some distaste and nodded grudging acknowledgement as we were introduced to each other. Our daughter glowered at them. I smiled, determined to preserve the courtesies, but they did not smile back.

The minister arrived, apologising, clutching sheaves of notes. He was a tall, handsome young black man, with a charming manner and a winning smile and, as you would expect, I was won over, if not instantly, within a few minutes of his taking his seat at the head of the table. You would have been won over too, as soon as you realised how well he had done his homework. He knew our application for legal aid had been refused and, unlike the men from the Legal Services Commission, he was sympathetic towards us. He listened attentively as each of us spoke to him. When I did my best to explain why we needed financial help to go to the High Court to get an admission of liability, making full use of the sad cases of the widow with the four children and the Taiwanese girl in hospital in Beijing, he shook his head and sighed understandingly.

He said, in a rich, gentle voice, "You must understand that I have no powers in this matter," his beautiful dark eyes resting sadly upon us. Then, turning his gaze to our adversaries but still speaking to us, "I understand that your original application for aid was perhaps a little premature. But I am quite sure if your solicitor were to apply again now, it would be more favourably considered."

For a man who had no powers, that sounded like a clear instruction to me. Our daughter was less convinced. "Too nice," she said, when the meeting was over. "That man from the legal services would eat him as an *amuse-gueule* before breakfast."

Our guide, who before he became an MP had been a lawyer specialising in physical-injury cases, touched my arm and said, "I would suggest you take Jarvis and Railtrack to the High Court on your own account and press for an admission of liability. It's my opinion that they'd give in at once. Even if they didn't, even if they won, which is almost inconceivable, they wouldn't dare ask for costs against you. The media would slaughter them. They haven't exactly got much of a reputation now."

This was satisfyingly true — though not necessarily helpful. The firm of Snakeheads who had been responsible for failing to maintain the points have had other failures. Like many public-finance initiative companies, they have fingers in most profitable pies, not only railway maintenance and renewal but schools and hospitals. Almost every day there is a story about some new outrage they have committed but they don't seem to care. Snakehead companies are not real companies with real purposes: they exist only to make money and, like hyenas and jackals that tidy up rotting meat, relieve governments of burdens they prefer not to carry. And in the end they cost the taxpayer more than if they were publicly funded.

Sorry to rant on. I am probably only telling you things that you always knew. It has often surprised me how much better *informed* you were than I have ever been about what went on in the world. Or at least more competent in finding your way over or around what seemed to me towering obstacles, but which were often of an absurdly minor nature. Like the time we were in Ankara and due to call on an eminent old gentleman, recently retired, but still a considerable figure in Turkish political life. You didn't have his address, you hadn't ordered a car. Although I didn't say so, in my view you were being carelessly casual in your approach to such an important visit, but when we left the hotel, a taxi was waiting, you opened the back door for me and said calmly to the driver, "Izmet Pasha."

Naturally, all was well. There are always free taxis in Ankara. And all drivers would know Izmet's address. But I was impressed that you knew this. Of course, your job had taken you out and about while mine kept me hunched over my computer, emerging occasionally to sniff the air and look up a fact in the British Library, giving me less chance to learn the ways of the world.

I hope I am catching up now.

Jarvis have just been awarded a three-million-pound contract to renew the stretch of track at Potters Bar where our train derailed, clattering over the defective points that killed you. Not a word of protest from the government. It is as if they are openly colluding with the Snakeheads in their refusal to accept responsibility for the crash. This is the private domain where policy is decided with a nod and a wink; where ordinary people

69

have no influence or power. And so I was not convinced that they wouldn't dare use every ounce of their legal muscle to beggar me if they got the chance.

I said, to this nice MP, "Maybe you're right. But I can't risk it."

I hate being so helpless.

The police have been to see me, as they said they would, along with a couple from the Health and Safety Executive who had travelled from Manchester. I gave them tea and coffee and cucumber sandwiches. Quite a social occasion. What the policeman in charge of the investigation had come to tell me was what I had suspected: the police were to hand over what they call "the primacy" of the investigation to the HSE. This didn't mean, he assured me, that they were giving up: they had merely come to a temporary stop. They had hoped to uncover clear evidence that the crash had been caused by Snakehead negligence in safety procedures, which would make it possible to prosecute the corporation for a serious criminal offence. Even if they could have determined who was actually responsible for failing to replace the bolts they didn't want to prosecute someone on the lowest rung of the line of command. The emphasis was now to be on looking at the company's policies and systems in which the HSE have specialist skills. They have also — I found this difficult to believe at first — more chance of getting the truth out of people.

The man from the HSE said, "I can always compel someone to talk."

"Cattle prods?" our daughter suggested.

He shook his head.

"How, then?" I asked.

He looked pleased, as if he relished this challenge. "I'll show you," he said. And then — you would have enjoyed that moment — this quiet, bespectacled, nice man from Manchester sat forward in his chair (the green King James chair you and I bought in Camden Passage with the *exact* money I earned on that book-promotion tour in America) placed his strong hands on his spread knees and became an inquisitor.

He started conversationally, almost casually: "Say someone in this factory I am investigating has lost a hand because the safety guard was not properly fixed across the machinery. There are four or five men involved. Not one of them can, or is willing, to tell me how the accident occurred. I take each one in turn into a small room. Just the two of us. We sit facing each other as I am facing you now. And I say . . ."

He leaned forward a little and the tone of his voice changed, became subtly menacing.

"*I want the truth. Anything you tell me will be in full confidence.*"

He paused. His pauses were theatrical, part of the act: he was not waiting for me to answer him.

"*Give me your name.*"

Pause.

"*Where do you live?*"

Pause.

"*How old are you?*"

Pause.

"Are you married?"

Pause.

"Do you have children?"

Pause.

"How long have you worked with this firm?"

Pause.

"What do you earn?"

A longer pause this time. Through his glasses his eyes remain steady. I am beginning to feel absurdly uneasy.

He says, more sharply, "Then I ask the key question — how did this happen? And he won't answer. Or he prevaricates. He can't remember. He had his back turned. He doesn't know who fixed the safety guard last. He doesn't remember there being trouble with it before. I wait. Then go on . . .

"You will have to tell me the truth. If you don't, you are committing a criminal offence. Did you know it was a criminal offence to obstruct my investigation?

"Well, it is. I can take you to court. You could be sent to prison.

"I repeat, it is a criminal offence. Not a mere civil matter.

"I would have no hesitation in doing so. I am used to taking people to court. I enjoy the whole process, in fact.

"All right. Good. Now we will start afresh, shall we? So — what is your name?"

The man from the HSE sat back in our green chair and beamed at us all.

I said, admiring but shocked, "I would have told you anything."

"The truth, I hope. You understand that this is not a method of investigation available to the police?" He sounded pleased with himself.

I said, "I had no idea . . ."

I was curiously comforted. I trusted this confident man.

I went to Greece for Easter with our daughter and granddaughter and our friend Liz, the three of them providing protection from the pain of not finding you there — not in the main square of Nauplion, not in the taverna at the bottom of the *scala*, not in our apartment. All the same, I still half expected to meet you around every corner, bringing news of Dimitri or Phaidon or Costas or Babis, or some just-discovered change in the town.

What alterations would you find now? More tourist shops as you might have expected but they are mostly cheap factory jewellers, nothing to threaten our skilled silversmith friends in Spiliadou. The blind shoemaker has gone, and although the bent old dressmaker who used to mend for us and turn the collars of your shirts for a couple of drachmas is still living in the small square near the church, her narrow slit of a shop where she sat with her sewing-machine now sells only collarless shirts with *I Love Greece* stamped on them. And Maria, our neighbour, whose great age convinced you that she must have been the first woman dentist in Greece, is still alive and in her house with the brass plaque on the door. She met me in the street and we shared the usual tearful embrace.

I wish my Greek was more adequate for these commiserating encounters of which there are many. You are remembered here. And much mourned.

We had a good week; bright and sunny, if cold. My three companions swam but largely, I guess, from bravado. We walked round the town and took the headland path to the beach. Liz walked to Karathona and back. I was happy with the three of them safely surrounding me, a welcome padding against my present anxiety. I had to make a decision during these few days away; I knew what it had to be, but I was unwilling to make it.

The Health and Safety Executive had yet to make their final report. I was still sure that my confidence in the good man from Manchester had not been misplaced but time was not on our side. It was almost two years since the accident, Railtrack and Jarvis had still not admitted liability or agreed any compensation, and any legal procedure against them had to be under way before the third anniversary. The minister I had seen at the House of Commons had spurred the Legal Services Commission into making an offer of aid, but of an impractical kind. They wanted to know the financial means of all the claimants; once they knew that, they would decide how much each of us should contribute towards the cost of applying for summary judgement in the High Court before they decided on how much they would stake us. We would all be in our graves (those of us whose ashes would not have been scattered) by the time this was done.

I might be unwilling, but knew that I had no real alternative but to take it on myself. Louise was convinced it was necessary, our daughter has always thought it was the only course of action and now our son agrees with her. So as we sat in the square, warmed by the sun shining through gauzy clouds, I sipped my ouzo and contemplated an old age in the gutter.

What would you do in my place? Oh, I know. Go to the High Court. Sue the buggers. It's only money. That's what you always said and you usually turned out to be right. *Only money*, you said, when I worried that we were spending too lavishly when we were furnishing our attic in Nauplion. *Money we haven't got*, was my view at the time but then I got a film option on one of my novels; they never made the film but it paid for the expensive hand-carved beds and chairs and dining-table we bought in Athens from that dark, rarely open shop on the edge of the Plaka.

Have I always been timid?

Trying not to think about what I was going to have to do after this sunny Greek interlude, I diverted myself with fiction, as always. I took as my starting point a middle-aged widower whose wife had survived the crash but died of her injuries some months later, leaving him not only desolate but haunted by jealousy. His wife's lover, who had been with her in the train, had been killed instantly and would now be with her in Paradise.

Tricky to make this convincing. It always depends on the telling. But I don't think I can do it. I would have to assume that the widower believes in life after death and

I don't think I can find it within me to make this plausible. Pity.

So this letter, which I know you will never read, but which comforts me to write, will stick to the facts. As far as my nature will let me.

We — I — have had a break-in. No, I hadn't put the alarm on; as you know, the thought of being woken by it at night has always frightened me. But I had locked the heavy fire door that shuts off the dining room and kitchen from the rest of the house, the door that the local borough surveyor insisted we install — against our wishes at the time. So when the burglars smashed the glass in the back door and used one of those fishing lines with a hook on the end that our daughter maintains are always carried by most young men in her part of London, although they were able to get hold of the key cupboard that we had foolishly nailed within reach and open the back door, the fire door defeated them. There was no spare key in the cupboard, and they couldn't push the key through from the kitchen because the door was too thick. Plastic sheeting that they had slid beneath the door to catch the key had been left behind. They had taken nothing except the neighbours' keys from the key cupboard; they had not touched the heavy Victorian silver we had bought with the money my parents gave us when we married, the silver that had gained in value so much over the years that we had often wished there was some way of letting my father know how much his ill-afforded wedding present was worth now.

Luckily for me, Stephen, the playwright, was here, sleeping in the top room, and came down to find the mess long before I woke. By the time I came down, yawning, ready for breakfast, he had telephoned my brother and our daughter. I rang the local police, who came quickly, but although that was consoling they didn't, as one might have expected, try to see where and how the villains had got up from the canal. The only further communication I have had from them is an offer of counselling from some victim-support group.

Curiously — at least, it seems curious to me — I have not been any more nervous than I was before. I think the idea of flesh-and-blood men breaking in frightens me less than the creaks in the old house at night, the imagined step on the stair. You would be proud of me now. I have had a new burglar alarm installed, the shutters on the first floor mended, and our daughter is ordering a folding grille for the fifth-floor back windows.

You were always more security conscious than I was. Why did you hide that old safe of your father's in the bookcase? We found a locksmith to open it and there are old keys inside, old letters, old photographs, and things like your paternal grandfather's birth certificate, which was issued in Hamburg although you always said your father's family came from Russia. I said you probably thought it more romantic to hail from Russia, but our daughter pointed out that the date on this certificate is some years after the year your grandfather was born. So perhaps the certificate was a fake to make it easier to get the family into South Africa.

FIVE

A week after we came back from Greece I gave an interview to Chinese Television. The company has a base in Chiswick and were making a programme about Potters Bar because the only survivor of the three girl friends from Taiwan, who had been travelling to Cambridge for a jolly weekend on our unlucky train, had been one of their anchor women.

Her injuries were horrific, to her liver, to her spine, to her ribs and, most seriously of all, to her skull, which was broken open. The famous London hospital she had been taken to said there was no hope for her, and one well-intentioned doctor suggested to her family that they should "let her go". Instead they summoned a neurosurgeon from China, who flew over to examine her and arranged for her to be taken to a hospital in Beijing. Within two months she had come out of her coma and, after a painful year of surgery, was able to stand by herself.

Her recovery was due, so the television presenter who interviewed me claimed, to a skilful combination of conventional and Chinese medicine, but it was so far only partial: I saw her later on another television programme, British this time, and her features were strangely rigid, her mouth distorted, making her speech slow and not very coherent. Watching her on the screen, bravely fighting to form words with her twisted mouth, it was hard to imagine she would ever work again in her chosen profession, although she insisted that she intended to.

I had not been interviewed by a foreign television company before and was not sure what to expect. The beaming and, surprisingly (for a Chinese I thought) tall and rotund cameraman, the young male presenter and a pretty girl, all of them charming and competent, arrived on the stroke of the hour they had engaged to arrive, and left precisely half an hour later as they had said that they would. They brought no flapping silver screens, no hugely bulging bags of equipment, no dazzling lights, and moved only one piece of furniture, replacing it when they had finished in the exact spot they had taken it from.

They wanted to know about my injuries. How was I managing without my husband? Had I received anything from the railway companies, any offer of compensation, perhaps a letter of regret? The young woman who was struggling to walk and talk in Beijing had heard nothing, which was why they were making this programme. I explained that the rest of the victims were in the same boat, and that the railways and the government had been disgracefully negligent. Then I did my best to explain the importance of establishing liability, which I think they understood, although they were more interested in how many of my bones had been broken and whether I was able to live a normal life on my own. But they were so delicately mannered that they allowed me to persist with my own agenda and I felt satisfied that at least some of my vitriolic views on the railway industry and the British government would be broadcast to the whole of China.

So I was nicely fired up to greet Tugboat Annie, who arrived shortly after they left. She is on an ambitiously roundabout journey, visiting friends on her way to Australia; she has decided to end her days in the country of her birth after a working life spent in the World Service followed by twenty years of retirement with Michael in Greece. She has been living alone there since he died, and although as you know she speaks excellent Greek and had successfully embedded herself in their small, remote village, she says that after a couple of years of widowhood, she found herself longing to speak her own language, be among her own kind. (You may be interested to know that "embedded" is a word we used to think, if we thought of it at all, as connected with horticulture. Since the Iraq war it is generally supposed to mean journalists living with, bedded among, the military.)

It was wonderful to see Annie, though sad to realise that some things are over for ever, that you and I will never again sit with her and Michael on their shady terrace, looking at that marvellous view and sipping the pungently intoxicating liqueur they make in the Pelion. When we went out to dinner at the Italian restaurant I asked Annie what the liqueur was called and she wrote it down for me on the back of my cheque book because

I didn't have my diary or any other useful piece of paper in my handbag. Tsiperou. Would you have remembered? I also found out, over a warm and gossipy meal, why you used to call her Tugboat Annie. I can't think how I could have forgotten that she ran the Merchant Navy radio programme while she was with the BBC. I suppose it didn't come into the conversation during our meetings in Greece when the four of us were busily living in the present, not looking back to the past, and so the memory slipped away like so many others. Not worth the storage space in the dusty attic of my mind? Unless I am losing my wits.

The next morning our sister-in-law telephoned before breakfast. Their post had come unnaturally early, which is to say that it had arrived at the time it always came in the happy days when we had two daily deliveries, and among the bills and junk mail was a letter from the chief executive of Network Rail to say that they and Jarvis are formally accepting liability for the crash. I was almost afraid to believe it, but the same miraculously good news was in my own post when it came at its now normal time of half past eleven. The admission was a trifle grudging, contriving to suggest that it was only being made because of the heart-rending concern the Snakeheads felt for the sorrows of the injured and bereaved, and it tried to make a false distinction between liability and responsibility, so that it might seem to the casual reader that the companies were not really culpable, but it was a greater relief to me than I would have liked to tell anyone. Now I was in no danger of the financial disaster I had feared was inevitable if I had to take the railways and their private contractor to the High Court to make them admit liability. (This action could not have been funded by the conditional-fee arrangement we had with our solicitors, and if I had lost I would have had to pay not only my own costs but the defendant's as well, and any compensation I was likely to get might not have been enough to cover me.)

I even felt, foolishly I think you would say, a little remorseful about my angry outburst on Chinese Television. I rang the company and was comforted by the graceful tact of the young presenter who managed — without making it clear that they had not really been interested in my tirade about the government and the railways — to explain that the programme, which had already gone out, had been edited to highlight my injuries and not my opinions. There was to be another programme later in the week and it would be "wonderful" if I would agree to appear on it and explain how the railway's acceptance of liability would be of such benefit to us all.

I do hope it will be. Louise is convinced that Network Rail and Jarvis were leaned on by the government, who are already in so much trouble elsewhere, mostly fallout from the foolish military adventure in Iraq, that they must have been anxious to avoid the bad press they would have received on the second anniversary of the crash, which was then only a couple of weeks away. I suspect there may be other factors. The chairman of Jarvis is standing for election as mayor of London and I imagine he would prefer that his connection with a firm still under investigation for negligence and possible corporate manslaughter does not become too prominent a feature in the campaign. And, of course, there is all our sterling campaign work, as well, perhaps, as an intervention by the minister.

Louise was — and is — properly angered by the weasel-worded way the admission of liability was handled. She had heard a rumour that the Snakeheads had been planning to announce their acceptance of liability to the press the week before, on the Friday evening, presumably in an attempt to bury the news at the weekend and before she or any of her clients had been told. They only agreed to delay it and send out the letters the following Monday after she had telephoned to complain.

I wondered what Gruff-voice would say. There have not been many meetings lately at which I would have expected to see him.

Louise intends to continue to press for a public inquiry. Since the Crown Prosecution Service has decided not to prosecute — unless evidence of criminal activity is later discovered — and the Transport Police have yielded what they call "primacy" to the Health and Safety Executive, the coroner has announced his intention of holding a full inquest into the deaths of seven people. Louise argued that previous rail crashes have all been the subject of public inquiries and the remit of a coroner would not include an investigation into how the contracting out of maintenance and the renewal of rails to private firms puts safety at risk. And the English inquest in its present form forbids the framing of a verdict in such a way as to determine civil or criminal liability so that it lays no blame at anyone's door.

I supposed she was right. All the same, at the time the thought of going on with the fight lowered my spirits. I thought it was over and that we had "won". A feeling of exhaustion descended and would have lain heavy on me, if it had not been for the reassuring presence of Tugboat Annie. When the calls began to come the moment the news was out, she stiffened my weakening resolve and nodded approvingly as I answered the telephone and said I was too busy to give interviews to anyone and, if she decided I sounded the least bit uncertain reminded me, with an inventive dumb show, that I had invited some retired and eminent BBC pundits for a reunion with her that very evening.

In the end I unplugged the telephone, but until I had drunk a couple of glasses of that good New Zealand Oyster Bay you used to like so much and which I now order by the crate, guilt kept a ghostly bell ringing in my ears. There was a dramatic storm that evening, thunder and lightning and a wild wind hurling torrents of rain against our swaying terrace of elderly houses until it seemed they might crack. The weather mirrored my inner turmoil but I think I managed to stop myself burdening your old colleagues and friends with my railway obsession. The trouble is, I find it difficult to take anything seriously apart from the train crash and the desert your death has left behind. I try to keep up with the news, but wars, famines, earthquakes, all pass as swiftly as an idly watched soap on the television. And, presumably, so I remind myself constantly, as major train crashes do for those not involved in them.

Anyway, the BBC evening went well. Joyful cries of *Tugboat! After all these years!* and fervent embraces. I can't remember what we ate, but we drank the Oyster Bay and Oxford Landing. I think you would have approved of my choice of wines. As you would have enjoyed the company.

The storm blew all night. In the morning the air was fresh and sweet as we went to the newsagent to pick up the morning papers, all of which carried the story of Network Rail's admission of liability and were mostly rejoicing on our behalf, although there was what (with a slight change of mind) I began to see as a disheartening suggestion that the matter was finished now and could be laid comfortably to rest.

The press, as I may have told you before, have been on "our" side all along. Their difficulty is that they need a peg to hang a story on, and at that moment the rest of our story seemed likely to be a touch uneventful. Even dull — except for the survivors, perhaps. Bargaining for decent compensation, Snakish tardiness on the part of the railways, total indifference from the government, and the Health and Safety Executive's reasons for deciding that a public inquiry would not be helpful might not make for the most sparkling piece of breaking news.

Annie sustained my spirits while she was with me. The morning she left I went to the physiotherapist who attempts to deal with the damage done to my skeleton in the accident, walked out of his office a little more upright and returned home to lunch with our daughter.

Afterwards, when she had gone — to walk her dogs, care for her house and her child — the grey depression that had been lurking all week closed in on me. It is obviously worse when I am alone; especially at night, in bed, when I put out my hand and find no one there. But it can descend suddenly, unexpectedly, any time, any place — like the men's clothing department on the ground floor of John Lewis in Oxford Street when you enter from Cavendish Square. I have never, to my recollection, bought, or been with you when you bought, any garment from that particular store, and yet whenever I go there I am assailed by such a choking sense of desolation as I pass the rows of excellent but unremarkable shirts, trousers and striped flannel pyjamas that I can barely breathe, let alone speak. I wonder if I should buy you something, a pair of socks, a tie? Would that lay your ghost, which has apparently chosen to haunt John Lewis?

Other places that you would expect to be more evocative do not have this effect. There seems to be no specialised location for grief. It seizes me in our terrace house when it is empty, but if someone else is there, even if they are only coughing on another floor, it is more bearable. And I am always afraid at night. So I have become a landlady, turning your ground-floor study into a bed-sitting room. My first official lodger was a charming Canadian, who was introduced by one of our friends; her sister, I hope, will come in the autumn. In between, friends who understand my foolish fears come to stay with me at night; Liz, our daughter, our granddaughters, Stephen, Charlotte the painter . . .

Of course you don't know Charlotte. I have to remind myself all the time that since you were killed there are people I have come to know whom you will never know, or not in this life. And, of course, there are things I long to tell you about some of those you did know, old friends who have fallen ill, published a novel, had a new baby. Freddie has died, for example, Freddie-next-door. He grew senile and his Danish family removed him to Denmark; he left on the day I came out of the hospital. A developer has bought his house and is noisily removing most of the features that made it beautiful. And Lily was born, the year of the accident. You would want to know these things, wouldn't you? Or am I only sad because I cannot tell you?

There is one thing that I know you would have liked me to tell you. The English Pen Club hold an International Writer's Day once a year at which various annual prizes are presented, and this year I was given a Gold Pen for a "lifetime's service to literature". A very pretty present, too, a gold pen on a stand and another gold pen for use. You will understand exactly how I felt about this, pleased, of course, proud, but embarrassed. Everyone said a great many complimentary things but I am not very good at receiving praise, as you know, and one of the minor reasons I wish you had been there is that I know you would have been graceful on my behalf.

90

I was given the prize in a remarkable venue for a writer's organisation: the Salvation Army hall in Oxford Street. What was remarkable about it was not the place itself, a decent hall with plenty of seating and adequate toilet arrangements, but the fact that, being the Salvation Army, the building was dry. No alcohol was served with the (very nice) sandwiches and the sight of a crowd of writers standing with cups of tea or orange juice instead of glasses of wine in their hands was unusual and comic. There was, of course, a fairly precipitate general exit to the nearest pub once the sandwiches were finished.

I tell you this because I don't want you to think my life is quite without pleasant diversions. Each evening, with one of my good companions, has its own shape. Some evenings we go out, to the theatre, the cinema, or invite people to dinner; other times we play Scrabble, or watch television, which, except for the news, I dislike watching alone. And since all these kind people loved you and miss you they endure my lecturing them on some new wickedness of the railway companies, or on some recent discovery I have made, a report by the Health and Safety Executive, or a hint of a scandal picked up from newspaper clippings that suggests that the Strategic Rail Authority would like to get rid of the HSE, which wants to impose safety measures that it judges too stringent for commercial prosperity.

When I cannot keep my obsession to myself, the David Hare play about the decline of the railways has been a useful resource. *The Permanent Way* is a splendid polemic that has been packed out since it opened but most of our friends have contrived to see it and are happy to talk about it. Before he started work, Hare came to see me with Kika Markham, the actor who was to play both me and Louise.

The play opened in York but then came to the National Theatre. I went to the first night in London with the family, who were, I think, anxious that I might be distressed by what was to take place on the stage. In fact I was rather more apprehensive of being unable to escape once I was imprisoned in a dark theatre. But from the beginning the play was so skilful that I ceased to be afraid: I was too absorbed. And I was not alone. When the last word was spoken the audience sat silent for a long, breathless moment. Then came the applause.

You will remember Hare's trilogy about the Church, the law and the Labour Party? This piece is done in the same way, actors playing a number of parts, changing a hat or a jacket on stage to establish their roles. Kika wore a neat black jacket when she was being Louise, and a remarkably pretty one in figured velvet when she was playing me. She had looked in my wardrobe and admired a jacket that came from an expensive local shop, but the company decided it was beyond their price range and Kika bought an effective and cheaper one from the Hampstead Bazaar. And when I admired it, she bought me one like it, which I wear with pleasure. You would have loved Kika.

The play has had rapturous reviews. The only sour comment came from a transport correspondent who objected because there was no solution offered to the dire state of the railways, an irrelevant criticism because the purpose of the play was to explain what this kind of catastrophe meant for those who were involved in it, for the dead, the injured, the rescuers, the train drivers, the guards, the inspectors of the tracks and the gangers who walked their lengths.

We all know what should be done about the railway system. Using Alistair Mant's analogy, it is a frog, not a bicycle. That is to say an organisation as complex as the railway system is not something that can be taken apart like a piece of machinery, which is what the Tory government did when they privatised it. A functioning, integrated railway is an organic being, like a frog. If you take a bicycle to bits to mend it, you can put it back together without damage, but if you cut the legs off a frog, the frog dies. Separate track from trains, split the railways into over a hundred different companies run for private profit, and you have lost the common purpose and safety culture that the old, integrated British Rail once had.

When I was at my elementary school in Dagenham, some of my friends' fathers were railwaymen and I don't think I am being nostalgic when I remember how proud they all were to work for the railways. One I particularly liked, because he mended my bicycle tyre for me without despising me for being unable to do it myself, was a lengthman; that is, a ganger who walked his length of track at least once a day. It was a low-paid job, he belonged to the lowest-paid group among railwaymen, but he was proud of it. I remember him saying, "As long as the track is safe, the train is safe, see? All those people's lives in my hands, that's what I tell myself."

No one walks the track regularly now. Railtrack contracted out maintenance to private companies, who employed few skilled railway engineers — some of their workers, indeed, were often no more than casuals drafted in for the day. Some of my pen-pals have horrific stories to tell of penalties they had suffered for exposing a fault that meant closing the line while it was repaired, of the drive for profit instead of safety. So broken fishplates, damaged points, cracked rails awaited the trains that thundered over them, killing and maiming passengers but seldom giving the contractors, the politicians and their advisers, who between them tore apart the railways, a single sleepless night.

Except for these Snakeheads, everyone who has anything to do with the railways knows this. Ordinary people know it, even if their complaints have more to do with punctuality and filthy seats and carriages than the danger to their lives. But our older granddaughter told me the other day that shortly after the accident she had a conversation with a British Transport Policeman, who said to her, "Don't you worry, we'll get them for this one."

Not so simple, as it turns out. The train crash that preceded ours — "ours" seems a silly word but it is the way I think of it — was the Hatfield crash in 2000. The fault then lay in a crack in the rail, which was diagnosed the morning after the disaster. The Health and Safety Executive are certain that badly maintained points 2182A at Potters Bar derailed our train. But there were eighty-three things wrong with those particular points so they have been unable to pin down the precise cause and effect clearly enough for the police to proceed to prosecution. Although eighty-three defects seem to me what you might call a positive contribution to potential disaster.

Do you remember the "rails" at Corinth? We discovered them when we climbed above the citadel of old Corinth — oh, years ago. I think we had already bought our apartment in Nauplion. One, or perhaps two of the children were with us. We saw these grooves cut into the rock and one of us said, "Rails. Like the railways."

I remember that they came to an end at the very edge of a steep, steep cliff and I was terrified because a child, one of the children, insisted on standing at the very edge with the precipitous drop a nudge or a stumble away so I can't remember if I joined in listening to the excellent explanation I am sure you would have been giving. I know I understood later that the Greeks moved their ships across the isthmus at Corinth on cradles with wheels that fitted grooves in the rock although I am still puzzled because the grooves we discovered by chance ran to the sheer edge of the cliff. Perhaps the rest of the cliff had fallen in the last two thousand years. Or perhaps there was a Greek rubbish truck that ran to the edge of the cliff on the same system and tipped the rubbish from the old town into the sea.

It seems like a dream now, our life together. I try to remember specific occasions: meeting you on

Hungerford Bridge in the early days when we were still married to other people, seeing you waving to me from a distance, then breaking into a run. Then, later, with the children and without them, in one house or another. Journeys we made. Travelling in Turkey with Canan, visiting that beautiful mosque in Konya. It was a particularly holy place so I covered my head with a scarf and wore a shirt with long sleeves to cover my elbows — elbows are considered very sexy in Turkey, you had warned me when I dressed in the morning. There was a group of giggly girls from Istanbul inside the mosque with us and an elderly Turkish gentleman accompanied by his shrouded wives. He looked at me and said something to the women, and Canan translated what he had said. "Look at the infidel. She at least has the decency to cover herself, while our girls dress like whores." I was so shocked. I said, indignantly, "I'm not an infidel," remembering one particular hymn we sometimes sang in school, at morning prayers. And you laughed at me!

We loved Turkey. But it was Greece that became our adopted country. I think of our first drive round southern Greece when we ran out of money and lived on bean soup. That was long ago, years before we even thought of buying an old house and living there.

But even our life in Greece is a dream. A happy dream but all the same not quite real, as at some level you always know a dream is not real. It is as if for memory to have the quality of reality it has to be verified. If I could say to you, "Do you remember the day we landed in Athens and were met by our lawyer and friend and told we could not buy our house because it had fallen down? And you said, we would buy it and build it up again, and she said, 'What? You buy air?' And we both said, in unison, that we would — to her horror." If I could ask you if you remembered that day and you could answer me, the past would be real again, solid, our flesh and blood selves moving and talking. Not drifting away like shadows when I try to touch them.

I have been re-reading your book about our comic tribulations when we did finally buy a house in Nauplion, in the old city. Only comic, perhaps, because they ended so well. I wish I could tell you that our lovely lawyer and John, our oldest Greek friend, have both been kind beyond measure since the accident, taking days from their busy lives to drive to and from Athens and Nauplion to help speed up the transfer of your half of our attic to our daughter. It saddens me that I have not yet seen them this year. I have a photograph of the four of us sitting at a taverna table, turning to smile at the camera. I look at it often but I cannot feel what I long to feel: the contentment of your being there, within reach . . .

SIX

Today, I am writing to you from Maine, sitting on the deck of the cottage that Liz rents every July on Long Pond. One summer you and I came here together. You would remember the loons on the lake, the red squirrels playing in the pines on the bank, the tiny, brilliant blue dragonflies. One has just landed on my notebook: about an inch and a quarter of narrow, glowing, transparent body and round black balls for eyes that appear to be watching me.

No English news here. Not much news of any kind. No television, no radio — although there is one in the cottage, I don't know how to tune to the World Service because you always did that. I might have done better if I had brought your short-wave radio with me, but once the railways and Jarvis had admitted liability I felt my task had been done: my part in the campaign for justice was successfully over. Just before I left for the States, flying to see our cousins in New York before coming here, I had made what I told myself was my last publicity effort, giving a joint interview with our daughter for the magazine of a widely read Sunday newspaper. We were interviewed, separately, in different rooms, by a pleasant woman journalist whose purpose, as frequently happens, was different from mine. I wanted to talk about railway safety and the general failures of the public-finance initiative and she wanted to know how our daughter and I got along together now she spends so much time with me, working as my personal assistant and secretary.

I told her that our daughter was wonderfully helpful and so efficient that she should really be running the country. And — what was really important to me at the moment — she shared my views on the iniquities of the government and the way they allowed the railways to be run. Her eyes, predictably, began to glaze over, and in an attempt to lighten things up a bit, I said that in the circumstances there was, inevitably, a certain amount of elder abuse.

Oh, I know, I know. This was one occasion when you emerged solidly from your hiding-place in the shadows. I swear I could hear you groaning at my elbow. I answered you in my head. "No one could take that seriously."

But of course, later, before I had a chance to speak to our daughter, a tactfully convoluted question was put to her when she was talking to the interviewer and I had retreated to my study. She was asked, "What do you think your father would say if he could speak to you now?" And our poor daughter, innocent, unwarned, laughed and replied, "I expect he would say, 'Don't bully your mother.'"

The week before I left London I missed an adjournment debate in the Commons on Potters Bar. I had been invited to attend but had allowed myself to be foolishly overwhelmed by other things I needed — or thought I needed — to do, and I regret missing it now. Apparently a brilliant and moving speech was made by the Member of Parliament for the constituency of the old lady who was killed when she walked under the bridge as the derailed train crashed into it. Luckily the debate was shown on television and our daughter-in-law has taped it for me.

I look forward to seeing it when they get back. (They are in Japan at the moment; our son describes the wonderful Japanese trains in an awed whisper.) Although I was relieved when I first got on to the plane at Heathrow at the thought of being out of the battle, safely out of reach, if only for a few weeks, I am now suffering quite severe withdrawal symptoms. Somewhat similar to those you experienced when you first retired, I imagine. No one, since I arrived in the States, has telephoned to ask my opinion! Othello's occupation gone! But it is also the lack of a daily injection of news. No newsagent, no corner shop, in this rural retreat. I seize on the *New York Times* when I can find it in one of the pretty little towns we visit occasionally, and alighted two days ago on a tucked-away paragraph in the business pages about the trouble Jarvis is in at the moment. I sent an e-mail to our son, who replied with a long article from the *Observer* about the company that they say "faces ruin, sinking under the weight of escalating debt and a shredded resolution. Some believe it is only a matter of time before vultures pick off the most lucrative contracts, leaving Jarvis a cash-strapped carcase."

Well, we will see. The company has been in trouble before and wriggled out of it. The banks, it seems, have given them to the end of the month to construct a survival plan. So there will be a fascinating cliff-hanger for the last few days of July when I get back to England. The firm has a stake in the Tube Lines consortium, the public-finance initiative chosen by the government to rejuvenate and run the Piccadilly, Northern and Jubilee lines; they can presumably sell this stake for a large sum of money. On the other hand, tales of the firm's incompetence had been appearing in the news almost daily before I left England. On one occasion they were fined heavily for a rail-repair blunder described by the judge as breaking a basic rule known to every child with a train set. "If you let a train run where there is no rail there will be a crash."

Network Rail, the public company that has taken over from the Railtrack, has begun to take back rail-maintenance work from the private contractors, which is a sensible step. But the government itself has shown no interest. Governments are not so unconcerned everywhere. My Australian brother has sent me the report on a rail crash that took place near Melbourne a few months after Potters Bar in which the same number of people were killed and almost the same number injured. But the prime minister was at the scene within four hours and a public inquiry announced within four weeks. And all the injured and bereaved were taken care of, helped, comforted and compensated before any inquiry took place and before any blame was allocated.

On the other hand, my obsessional perusal of the *New York Times* has led to the far-from-astonishing discovery that the railroads and the authorities in America are as negligent of human life as they are in our country, side-stepping blame in much the same way. There was a long report in the *NYT* on two successive days about deaths on rural level crossings and how the families left behind have had no help either from the railways or the federal government. The mother of a boy who was killed at one rural crossing, where six other people had died earlier, is reported as saying, "We are fighting a war with wounded soldiers here."

As you would expect from driving through the countryside, the cause of the deaths is often vegetation growing too thickly around the warning signs. Or, sometimes, the warning signs are themselves defective. When one man, driving a truck of potatoes to market, was killed on a crossing in South Washington State, the Union Pacific Railroad Company naturally blamed the driver. They did not admit — equally to be expected — that the warning signals at the crossing contained parts that the manufacturer had said, twelve years earlier, should be replaced "as soon as possible". A lawyer for the family arranged to inspect the signals but before he could do so a railroad manager had replaced the parts for newer ones. Luckily for the family, they had a smart lawyer who looked at the serial numbers on the new parts and saw that they did not match the railroad's records.

So they should get decent compensation, which, I suppose, will be the final stage of the struggle when this peaceful interlude is over and I am back in London. In the meantime I try to bring back our time here together, the year we came to Maine. We swam in the lake. We walked in the thick woods — full, you insisted, of goblins and trolls. We walked on the bare, breezy top of Mount Cadillac. We went to an excellent restaurant called the Burning Tree. Above all, you would have remembered the lobsters. Wonderful Maine lobsters that we bought steamed and cracked and wrapped in newspapers to keep warm as we drove back to the cottage where you and I and Liz ate them, looking out at the evening sun sparkling on the lake. Sometimes we heard the loons crying. That strange, sad, haunting cry.

Back in London there are no loons, only seagulls flying up the canal from Limehouse Reach and shrieking high in the sky. Family all still out of the country, street empty, most residents departed for their cottages — or castles — in the country. The usual August desolation. Even Louise is away. But, then, I have been out of reach too, in my rural retreat. Our daughter, however, never turns off her mobile phone in case she is needed — by her daughter, by her mother. Now she telephones from Greece. This last ten days, sitting on a beach, she has been rung by a television company as well as several newspapers asking for comments on several events, rumours, developments. Would she be prepared to stage a protest in Croydon? *Croydon?* Apparently a vast and hugely expensive new building to accommodate the bureaucracy that will in future deal with tedious details, like complaints and compensation claims, is to be opened there by the Transport Minister. And the government have issued a white paper detailing their intention to remove the safety regulation from the Health and Safety Executive in the kind of language only used by this kind of document. A sample word would be "interface".

But what exercises our daughter most has been an announcement from Network Rail, relayed to her by one of the newspapers, that they will limit compensation payments to five out of seven families of those killed at Potters Bar to the amount the law has decreed for the deaths of people who have no dependants. These are usually, of course, the old and the young. Although the two Taiwanese girls who died with you were in their late twenties, they had no children and were not supporting their parents.

Ten thousand pounds is the legal value of a negligently taken life, of a child or a parent. A cold and somewhat mean-spirited calculation: you would do better if you slipped on a paving-stone and broke a front tooth, particularly should you live in America. I used to disapprove of the "compensation culture", but experience has tempered my disapproval considerably. Making people responsible, for the cracked paving-stone they should have replaced or for the bolts that should have secured points 2182A, might make them more careful.

Obtaining compensation for injury rather than death is more of an obstacle race. I am not likely to recover much more and will need, I am told, some support for the rest of my life. But it is not enough to have been rendered unconscious and raving with legs, arms and ribs broken: evidence of continuing damage has to be proved by expensive medical specialists who are employed by the lawyers to read and report upon almost all a victim's medical history. I was not expected to admit the tonsillectomy that I endured in my early twenties, or the broken wrist I sustained when I came off my bicycle free-wheeling down a lane in Shropshire on the night of my eighteenth birthday, but in general, the legal teams on both sides have the right, or so it seems to me sometimes in my meetings with orthopaedic surgeons, psychiatrists, neurologists and the like, to investigate my whole life both physical and emotional: my earnings as a writer, my banking history, my shopping and eating habits, all of which I feel sure must be summed up somewhere under the heading of "lifestyle choices". No one seems interested in what your absence means for me practically, which seems to me pertinent — what you could be doing for me, what we could do for each other. Once or twice I have tried to point out that I would not have needed a night nurse for so long if you had been there to help me out of bed when I needed to go to the bathroom, or indeed, to cook a meal for me now: you were a better cook than I ever was.

But this is not logical. I would not have needed you to do these practical things for me because I would not have been on that particular train without you. We were going together to a party.

After visiting me in the hospital one evening, our son and several others went to an Indian restaurant. After they had ordered, he sensed there was something strange about the shape of the place and it slowly dawned on him that it was arranged and decorated as if it were a railway carriage . . . And he reports that on one occasion his train to London from Diss moved around two hundred yards before it ground to a halt. It was towed back to the station. When our son asked the engineer what had happened he told him, "There is a problem with the engine which they have known about for weeks."

The first time I travelled by rail after the accident was with your American cousins who came to London and took me to Paris. It was an imaginative thing to do. I was afraid in anticipation but they were determined. The young woman who was making the film about Potters Bar accompanied us with a cameraman. I felt I was expected to show fear and dismay but, perversely, all I felt was amusement. I explained what I thought they must think was a failure by saying that Eurostar, to my mind, was more of a magic carpet than an ordinary train.

Since then, the railways seem determined to teach me a lesson. I went by train with Liz to visit friends in the Lake District. The train slowed to a halt between stations. After a few long moments the train manager — that is what guards are called now — came on the speaker and told us that a microlight had landed on the line ahead of us and we would have to wait until it was removed. I cannot remember how long we waited but I know that no one in my carriage spoke, simply continued to read their newspapers and magazines or stared out of the window with calm, expressionless faces as if this was a normal event on a railway journey.

And coming back one late afternoon after visiting Phoebe in Bristol, the train juddered and shook so alarmingly for about twenty minutes that I was moved to speak about it to the man — the train manager? — who came to inspect my ticket. He said, oh, yes, it was always like that on this stretch of track: he called it the Bristol Bounce. I suggested he should report it and he laughed and said it would be a waste of time.

"They never do anything, do they?" he said.

ENVOI

There is no true end to this story. There will be months of argument over claims, brief flashes of public interest, but unless there is another train crash we are unlikely to hit the headlines again. Our younger granddaughter and Stephen think something more is needed to finish this letter. Something more than To be continued . . .

Some sort of farewell? I don't want to say goodbye to you. A summing up of our life together? A memory we once shared that is fading from my mind, the only lodging left to it now you are gone? Where will it go? What happens to the contents of a brain when the cogs and wheels stop whirring?

Would you like to know about the meeting we have just had with the Secretary of State for Transport? Although he was not en poste at the time of the accident, this was something the families that have been offered an insultingly small sum in compensation for the deaths of unproductive sons, daughters and old mothers had especially wanted. I thought it was unlikely to be useful but went all the same, and was charmed by a man as unlike a Snakehead as I could have imagined, even to the extent of imagining that he was sympathetic to our cause. Who can tell? You would have been better able to judge him. I wish you'd been there.

As I do all the time.

And perhaps, after all, you are still around somewhere, watching and listening. I think of the walking sticks . . .